100
PAPER Folding
projects

nuinui

Table of Contents

Chapter 4: Animals

Chapter 5: Moving Toys

Chapter 6: Chameleons Toys

Kim Jae Eun

(Ph.D. in Literature; Professor Emeritus in the Department of Psychology, Ehwa Woman's University; President of the Korean Educational Psychology Association; Board Member of the Korea paper Culture Foundation & World Jongie Jupgi Organization; and certified Korean paper-folding instructor)

Who is Mr. Kim Young Man? Everybody recognizes his name as he is a master of paper folding and paper sculpture as well as an extraordinary author and popular TV personality. He has been teaching innovative paper-folding techniques for over 20 years on television shows such as KBS TV Kindergarten One, two, three, I'm Doing Well by Myself, and EBS Dingdongdang Kindergarten. More recently, he has appeared on MBC TV My Little Television.

Simply put, Kim Young-man is a superb instructor, entertainer, and social activist. Along with Roh Young-hye, Chair of the Korea paper Culture Foundation, who has helped organize paper-folding and paper-promotion campaigns throughout Korea, he has traveled to many countries to spread the message of world peace through paper folding.

Jongie Jupgi Mr. Kim Young-man's paper-Folding Projects is an excellent manual on the fundamentals of paper folding. The book promotes the idea that paper folding has wonderful psychological benefits both for those practicing it on their own and those doing it in the company of others, with whom they can exchange tips and stories.

The text is simple and accessible to everyone from preschoolers to grandparents. Indeed there's no need to read the instructions as the illustrations alone can teach you how to fold paper anywhere – at home, in kindergarten, day-care centers, camping grounds, schools, trains, senior and youth centers, and nursing homes. The book offers easy and enjoyable projects. I personally, recommend it highly!

paper folding is not just a simple game, but a means of stimulating the brain. Research shows that it can help prevent and even treat dementia. It is a fascinating pastime for the entire family, and an enjoyable form of recreation that involves both innovation and meticulous manual coordination. It offers emotional support and nurtures a sense of belonging.

I hope this book will bring joy to readers. The concentration demanded by paper folding and paper crafts brings peace. A few sheets of origami paper are all that's needed to generate joy. It's up to you whether you wish to indulge!

Materials and Tools

Paper-folding with Mr. Kim Young Man does not require many supplies.
Origami paper, glue, and scissors are all you need.

Origami paper

Find vivid origami paper that reflects your personal creative flair.

Colored paper

Colored paper comes in a range of hues and patterns (vivid or embossed patterns, as well as various sizes and weights: 100 g, 120 g, 150 g, and 190 g).

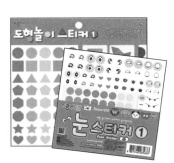

Stickers

Choose stickers that match your creative style.

Crayons

When rubbed with a finger, soft and colorful crayons will have a pastel-like quality. If applied with a wet brush, they work like watercolors.

Glue stick

Glue should be strong and highly adhesive.

Safety scissors

Even young children can use scissors with a safety hook.

Basic Symbols and Instructions

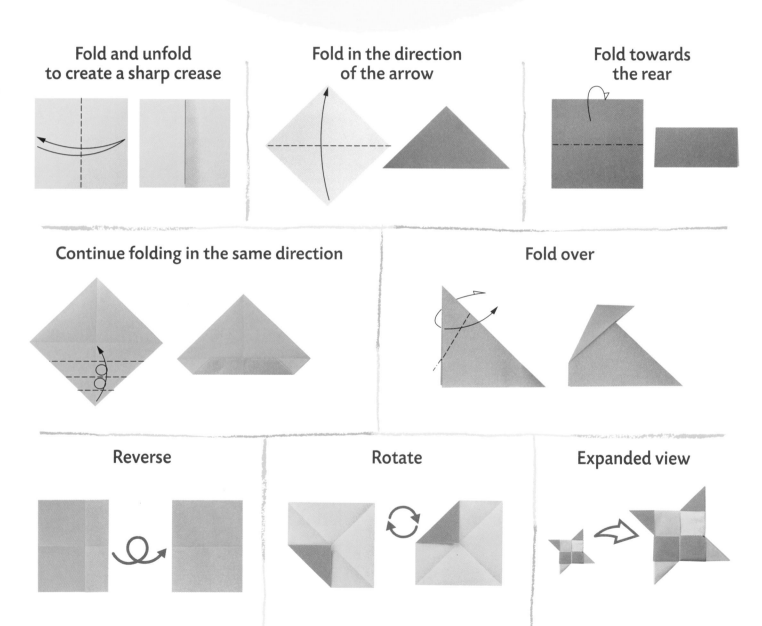

Fold and unfold to create a sharp crease

Fold in the direction of the arrow

Fold towards the rear

Continue folding in the same direction

Fold over

Reverse

Rotate

Expanded view

Basic Folding Methods

Folding a magic wand

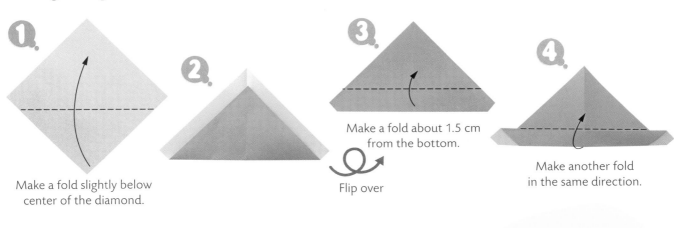

1. Make a fold slightly below center of the diamond.

2. Flip over

3. Make a fold about 1.5 cm from the bottom.

4. Make another fold in the same direction.

5. Make another fold in the same direction.

6. Glue the tip down to create a straight wand

Joy — Completed

Accordion Fold

Place two thin strips of different colored origami paper perpendicularly to each other

Fold the end of one strip over the other.

Fold one strip over the other.

Repeat the process until reaching the desired length.

Chapter 1
Paper Projectiles

Paper projectiles are meant to be thrown as far as possible.
Let's toss our worries away, and let Master Kim Young-man
teach us how to put our hopes and dreams
into paper-folding!

Have Fun with Paper Folding!

It just so happens that I appeared online for the first time on MBC's "My Little Television". This online TV show lets viewers post comments, so it was also my first time chatting online. One day somebody wrote "It's difficult to fold paper." I replied, "Get your Mom to help." The person then responded by saying that she had just become a mother.

When I asked online visitors "How do you make a living?" I discovered that some were college students while others were office workers. I told those who were doing a good job, "That's great! Thanks for posting comments and for doing a good job." Many friends, however, replied with a "ㅠㅠ", a Korean way to express sadness. This response brought tears to my eyes. My heart was heavy because many of our efforts are not adequately appreciated. When this episode of the show was ranked #1, I could not suppress my emotions and cried again.

But for now, let's toss our cares away and put our dreams and hopes into paper folding. Let's have fun, be happy, and do paper folding with our children or even our entire family!

It's easy

Spinning Loops

Make loops out of sheets of origami paper and glue them to each other. Magically, they become whirligigs that go round and round as they drop to the ground. By decorating them with paper cut-outs, you can turn them into birds. Decorate them with fun and interesting shapes!

Now, let's throw it up in the air!

Spinning Loops

One sheet of 15 × 15 cm, double-sided origami paper

1.
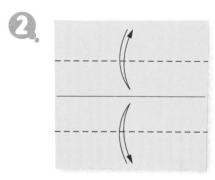

Make sure you press down hard on the fold!

Fold a square sheet of origami paper in half, then unfold to make a crease along the center.

2.
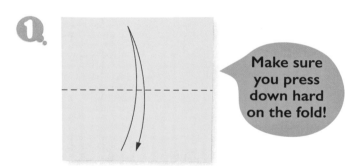

Fold and unfold each half of the sheet to create four creases of equal length.

4.

Shape after cutting.
You'll have four skinny rectangles.

3.
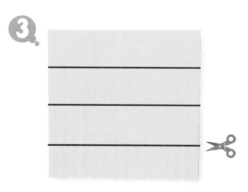

Cut along the lines.

(Loop)
Make four loops.

Use glue to connect the four loops.

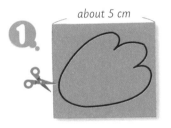

Apply glue to the shaded area and join to the other end to make a loop.

Bird-Shaped Spinning Loops

Three sheets of 5 × 10 cm, single-sided origami paper
One sheet of 7.5 × 7.5 cm, single-sided origami paper

When you complete a work, shout "joy" three times as it is fun and exciting! Joy! Joy! Joy!

Use your imagination to create a new shape.

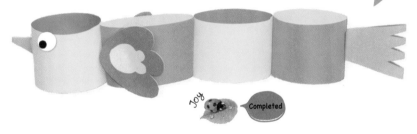

Decorate the loops with the beak, wings, and tail to turn them into a bird.

1.
about 5 cm

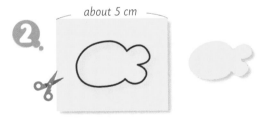

Fold a 5 × 10 cm sheet of origami paper in half, draw a small wing, and cut it out.

2.
about 5 cm

fold a 5 × 10 cm sheet of origami paper in half, draw a small wing, and cut it out.

3.

Glue the small wing onto the big wing.

4.
about 5 cm

Fold a 5 × 10 cm sheet of origami paper in half, draw a tail, cut it out, fold the edge, and glue it down.

5.

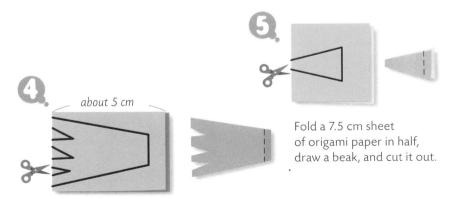

Fold a 7.5 cm sheet of origami paper in half, draw a beak, and cut it out.

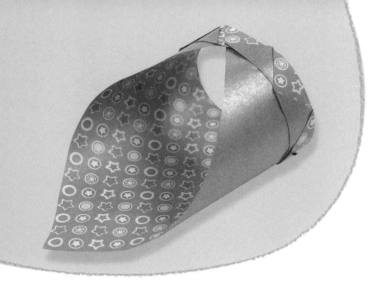

UFO 1

Little friends!
Paper-folding combines math, science, and art and represents wisdom and peace. Make a UFO with a sheet of double-sided origami paper to boost your scientific curiosity and fulfill your dream of becoming an astrophysicist!

One sheet of 15 × 15 cm, double-sided origami paper

4.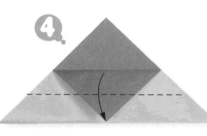

Fold the flap over itself.

1.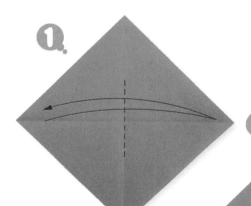

Fold in half and unfold.

2.

Fold bottom half towards the top.

3.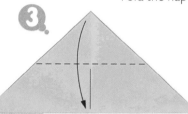

Fold the front half of the sheet down to the bottom edge.

a square sheet of origami paper turned into a triangle.

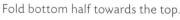

5.

Fold the bottom flap over itself a second time.

6. Keep folding the front half of the sheet along the folded lines.

7. Glue the shaded area to the other end.

Whenever somebody finishes a model, make sure to praise them regardless of whether they're adults or children. "Good job!" "Fantastic!"

Joy   Completed

Hi, my little friends! Smile and toss it up in the air! Toss your worries as far as possible!

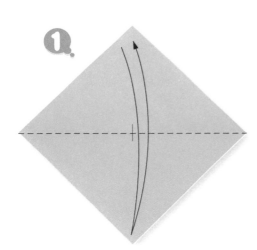

UFO 2

Fold paper to create a different spacecraft!

Spacecrafts! That's what science is all about!

Two sheets of 15 × 15 cm, double-sided origami paper

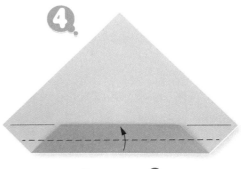

Repeat step **3**.

1.

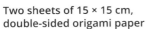

Fold in half and unfold.

2.

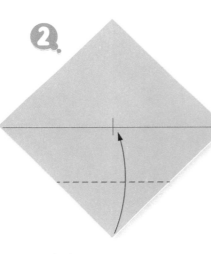

Turn the bottom corner up to meet the central crease and press down to make a fold.

3.

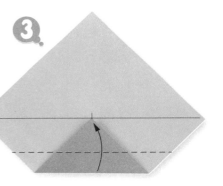

Fold the bottom edge over itself towards the central crease.

Master Paper-Folding Artist, Kim Young-Man, you are the best!

Make sure to press down hard on the fold!

5. Repeat step **3** one more time.

6. Folded shape.

7. Repeat the steps on the second sheet of origami paper. Apply some glue to the shaded area, bring this corner around and join it to the opposite corner by slipping it into the fold.

Joy Completed

Decorate with stickers. Pick the UFO up by the corner (where the black dot • is) and toss up in the air.

Ta-da! Joy!

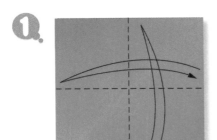

Space Rocket!

Dream! Show your talent!
Let's fold paper into a rocket that stimulates
your human creativity!

Two sheets of 15 × 15 cm, double-sided origami paper

1.

Fold each of the sheets
in half vertically, then
horizontally, and unfold.

2.

Fold each of the sheets
in half diagonally,
first from one side,
then from the other.
Unfold.

3.

Fold sheets in half from top to
bottom. Fold the top left and top
right corners down to meet the
base of the vertical centerfold.

4.

The triangular pocket is now completed.
Fold only the left and right front sides
down along the centerline.

4.

Fold the left and right sides of the front
of the triangle to the centerline.
Do the same on the rear.

5.

5.

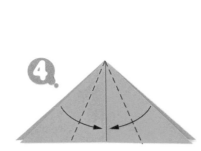
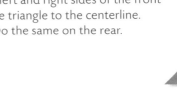

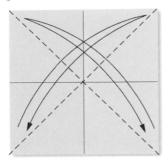

6. Insert one folded sheet into the other, following the arrows in the illustration.

6.

7. Appearance of model after one folded sheet has been inserted into the other.

8. Glue decorations on the rocket.

Joy — Completed

Imagine a fantastic sky and add a rocket!

Swoosh! Let's launch the rocket into outer space! Where is Mars, the planet closest to Earth?

Rocket Arrow 1

Make an arrow and shoot it as far as you can.
Grab the shaft and throw hard. Woosh!
Try to hit the target! Enjoy a game of shooting
and catching the rocket arrow!

Five sheets of 15 × 15 cm, double-sided origami paper
Two sheets of 7.5 × 7.5 cm, single-sided origami paper

Follow steps **1**-**4** on page 16 to make a triangle pocket.

1.

2.

3.

Make a second triangle pocket,
and insert it into the first one,
as shown in the picture.

Joy **Completed**

5.

Wrap one more wand around the other two
to make the shaft stronger, and secure with glue.

Make two more triangle pockets with the two sheets
of 7.5 origami paper. Insert them into each other
as shown in step **3**. Then insert and glue them
onto the front end of the wand as shown.

4.
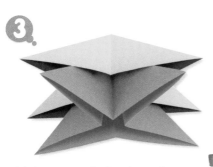

Following instructions on page 7, make two
15 × 15 cm magic wands. Insert one into
the other as shown, and glue them together.

Rocket Arrow 2

Wow, fantastic!

The rocket arrow's long tail makes it even better!

Five sheets of 15 × 15 cm, double-sided origami paper
Two sheets of 7.5 × 7.5 cm, single-sided origami paper

1.

Cut a corner out of a sheet of origami paper, as shown.

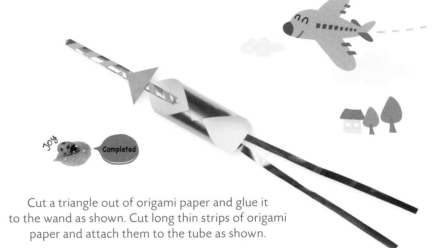

Cut a triangle out of origami paper and glue it to the wand as shown. Cut long thin strips of origami paper and attach them to the tube as shown.

2.

Pull one corner of the sheet to the opposite one and glue it in place to create a tube, as shown.

3.

Make a magic wand, according to the instructions on page 7, and glue it to the tube, as shown.

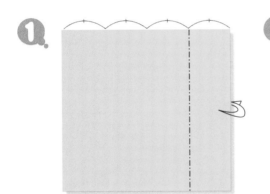

Spiral Rocket

The spiral rocket does twists and turns in the air before landing!

One sheet of 15 × 15 cm, single-sided origami paper

1.

Fold down one quarter of the sheet, then unfold.

2.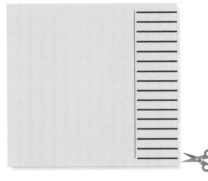

Cut narrow strips of equal width between the edge of the paper and the fold, as in the image.

3.

Fold down the opposite corner, as shown in the picture.

Good!

4. Apply glue to the shaded section and roll the sheet up into a cone.

5.

Joy Completed

Binoculars

Attach some colored cellophane to the front of the binoculars to create shaded lenses.

3. Apply glue to the shaded area. Glue that end to the one opposite to create a loop.

2. Make a narrow fold along the top of each sheet.

Two sheets of 15 × 15 cm, double-sided origami paper

1. Fold the sheet in half, then unfold and cut along the crease.

Throw the binoculars up in the air and they will spin round and round!

4. Make another loop with the second sheet.

5. Now both lenses are ready.

6. Follow the directions on page 7 to make a magic wand. Apply glue to the shaded area and attach it to both the binocular lenses.

Hold the binoculars up to your eyes to look into the distance!

Joy — Completed

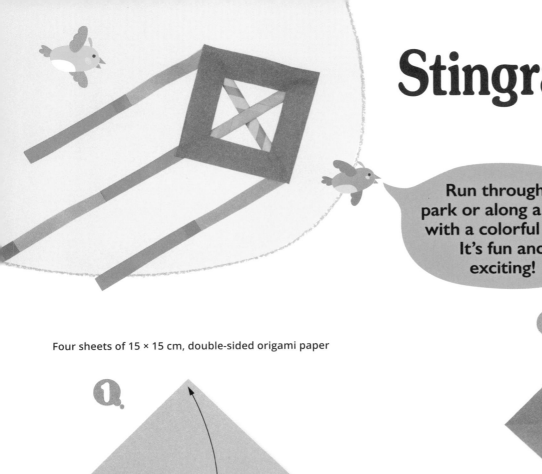

Stingray Kite

Run through a park or along a river with a colorful kite. It's fun and exciting!

Four sheets of 15 × 15 cm, double-sided origami paper

1.

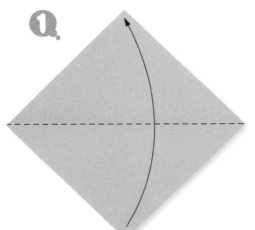

Fold sheet in half.

2.

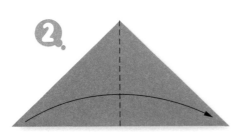

Fold in half again.

3.

Cut the triangle as shown.

4.

Unfold the entire sheet.

5.

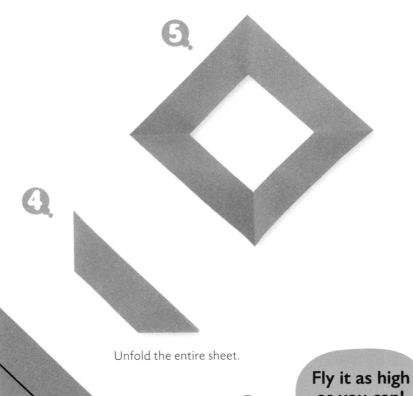

Fly it as high as you can!

24 ★★★

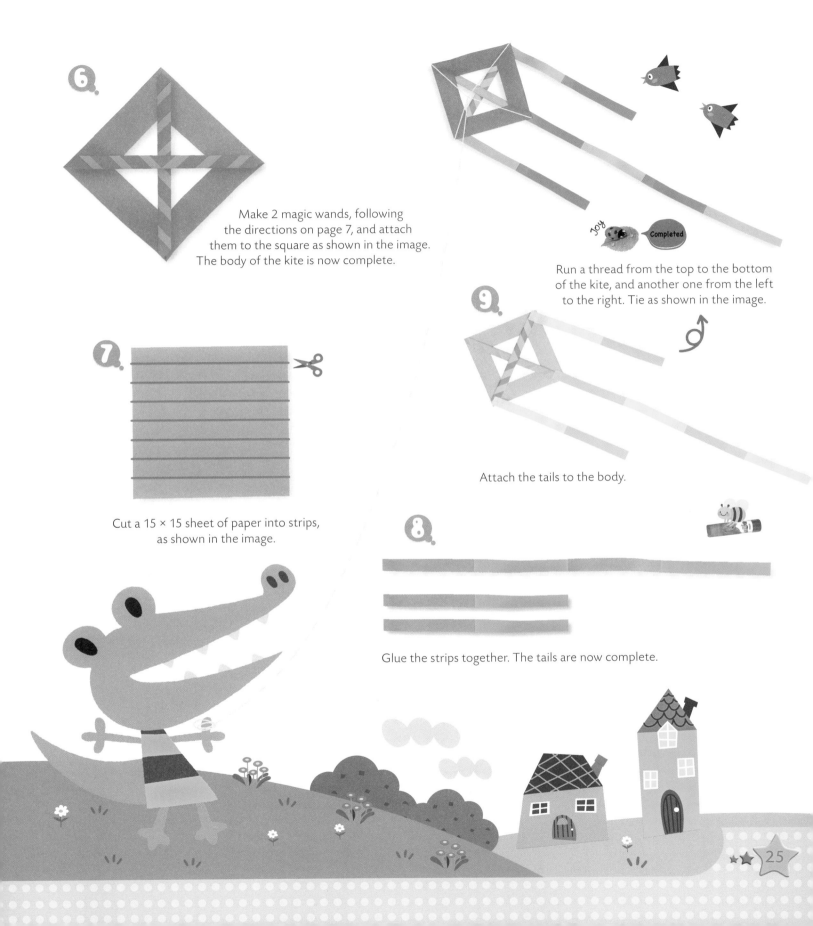

6. Make 2 magic wands, following the directions on page 7, and attach them to the square as shown in the image. The body of the kite is now complete.

Run a thread from the top to the bottom of the kite, and another one from the left to the right. Tie as shown in the image.

7. Cut a 15 × 15 sheet of paper into strips, as shown in the image.

9. Attach the tails to the body.

8. Glue the strips together. The tails are now complete.

Boomerang 1

Grab one of the legs, and fling it far into the sky!
Woosh, it's a gorgeous boomerang!

Woosh, let it fly!

Three sheets of 15 × 15 cm, double-sided origami paper
One sheet of 10 × 2 cm, single-sided origami paper

1.

Follow directions on page 7 to make three magic wands.

2.

Use the scissors to snip both ends.

3.

Glue the three magic wands at the center, arranging them as shown in the image.

4. Apply glue to the shaded area of the 10 × 2 cm sheet of paper and attach to the other end, to make a loop.

5. Apply glue to the shaded area of the wands, and attach the loop.

My friends! The Korean word for paper (*jongi*) derives from *joi*, or *joy* in English. Whenever you complete a project, cry out "joy!" to express your excitement!

Joy

Completed

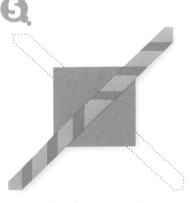

Boomerang 2

Three sheets of 15 × 15 cm, double-sided origami paper

Apply glue to the shaded area and fold the sheet in half.

Once you finish your boomerang, you can use it to play games with your friends!

Apply glue to the shaded area and fold the sheet in half.

4.

Make two magic wands following the instructions on page 7.

5.

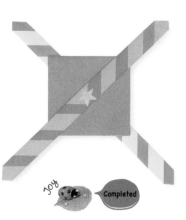

Glue the two wands at a diagonal to the square body, as shown in the image.

Completed

Wow, fantastic!

It's also fun using a round sheet of paper!

Winged Cup 1 & 2

Winged Cup 1

Two sheets of 15 × 15 cm, double-sided origami paper

1.

Be careful when handling the paper cutter! Do it with a parent at your side!

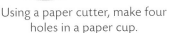

Using a paper cutter, make four holes in a paper cup.

2.

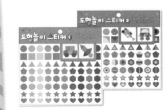

Make two magic wands, following the instructions on page 7.

3.

Insert magic wands into the holes in the cup and decorate them with round stickers.

Two sheets of 15 × 15 cm, double-sided origami paper

Winged Cup 2

Make a different winged cup using heart-shaped stickers.

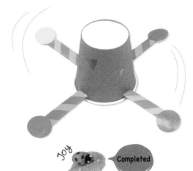

Tuho (Tossing Game)

Tuho is a tossing game in which two players compete by trying to get arrows into a basket. The player who gets the most arrows into the basket, wins.
The basket can be beautifully decorated.

Arrow

Multiple sheets of 30 × 30 cm, double-sided origami paper

Multiple sheets of 7.5 × 7.5 cm, double-sided origami paper

Fold a 7.5 × 7.5 cm sheet of double-sided origami paper in half and cut along the fold to create the feather, as shown in the image.

Arrow completed!

1.

Roll 30 × 30 cm paper from right to left.

2.

Apply glue to the shaded area and roll all the way to the end.

3.

Glue the feather to the end of the arrow.

Arrow Basket

One sheet of A4 double-sided origami paper

Cut the edge of the sheet with scissors, as shown in the image.

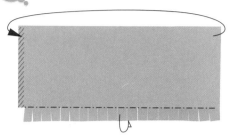

Apply glue to the shaded area and attach the opposite edge to create a cylinder.

Cylinder completed!

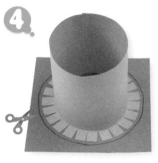

Glue the bottom of the cylinder to a 15 × 15 cm sheet of origami paper and cut the edge of the sheet to make a round bottom.

The arrow basket is completed!

Stand three or four steps away from the basket while aiming the arrows at it!

Decorate the arrow basket with stickers or colorful paper cut-outs.

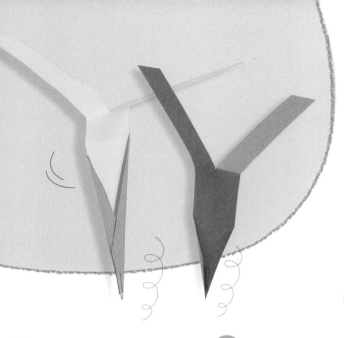

Helicopter 1 & 2

Helicopter 1

One quarter of a 15 × 15 cm sheet of double-sided origami paper

1.

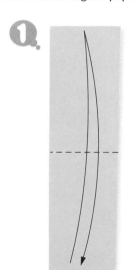

Fold in half, and unfold.

2.

Fold at the angle shown in the image.

3.

Fold at the angle shown in the image.

4.

Fold in the opposite direction.

5.

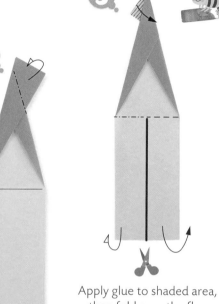

Apply glue to shaded area, then fold over the flap and glue the point down. Cut along the line of the bottom half, as shown, and fold the two propellers in opposite directions.

Completed

Helicopter 2

One quarter of a 15 × 15 cm sheet of double-sided origami paper

1.

Fold and unfold as shown.

2.

Fold the top right corner towards the central fold. Using scissors, cut the bottom of the central fold, as shown.

3.

Fold the top right corner again, as shown.

4.

Turn the sheet around and fold the top right corner in the same way.

5.

Fold the two propellers at the bottom in opposite directions.

It's spinning!

Throw the helicopter up into the sky and it will come spiralling down!

Joy   Completed

Paper-Clip Airplane

One sheet of 15 × 15 cm, double-sided origami paper

Fold in half and unfold.

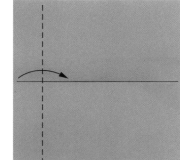

Make a narrow fold along the left edge of the sheet, as shown in the image.

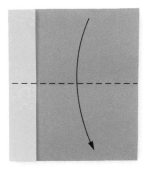

Fold in half from top to bottom.

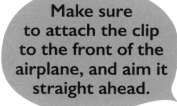

Make sure to attach the clip to the front of the airplane, and aim it straight ahead.

4. Cut as in the image.

5. Unfold.

6. Insert a paper clip, as shown.

Decorate the plane with stickers.

Wow, fantastic!

Yes!

Completed

Airplane

When folded, it flies beautifully and lands gently.
Place your dreams on this airplane
and make them soar!

One sheet of 30 × 30 cm, double-sided origami paper

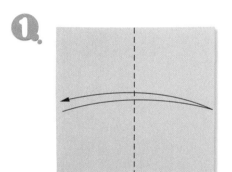

1. Fold in half and unfold.

2. Fold outer edges towards the centerline and unfold.

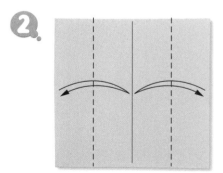

3. Fold outer edges to the creases made in step **2**.

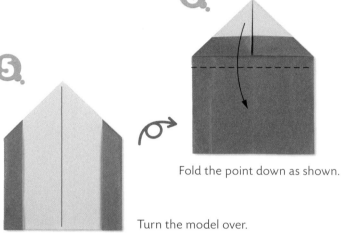

4. Fold top corners backwards down to the center line.

5. Turn the model over.

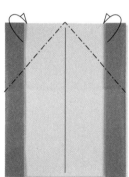

6. Fold the point down as shown.

7. Fold along the centerline.

8. Fold the tab as shown.

9. Flip the model over.

10. Fold sides back, as shown.

11. Fold model in half, as shown.

12. Fold along the dotted line, as shown in the image.

Lift up the wings on either side.

Joy Completed

The plane will fly longer if you throw it upward at 80 degrees. It will fly further if you throw it hard at 30 degrees.

Wow, fantastic, isn't it?

Make sure to bend your knees slightly before extending your arm forward and releasing it!

37

Flying Squid

Bend your knees slightly before thrusting your arm forward and letting the magic wand fly!
Swoosh, the flying squid will soar!

Magic wand completed!

Make two magic wands.

Magic Wands
Two sheets of 15 × 15 cm, double-sided origami paper

1.

Make a fold from the bottom up, a thumbnail's width away from the corner at the top.

2.

Flip model over to the other side.

3.

Make one fold after another, rolling up the sheet from the bottom up.

4.

Apply glue to the shaded area and attach the corner to the wand.

Clap your hands!

Ta-da! You can do it!

Squid

Two sheets of 15 × 15 cm, double-sided origami paper

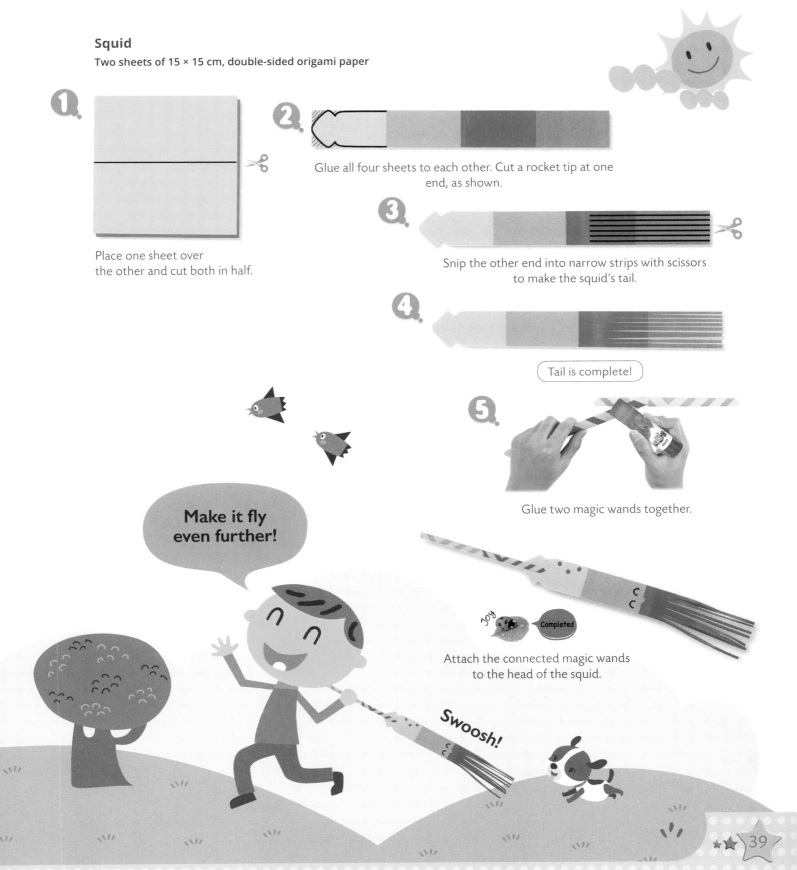

1. Place one sheet over the other and cut both in half.

2. Glue all four sheets to each other. Cut a rocket tip at one end, as shown.

3. Snip the other end into narrow strips with scissors to make the squid's tail.

4. Tail is complete!

5. Glue two magic wands together.

Attach the connected magic wands to the head of the squid.

Make it fly even further!

Swoosh!

Joy   Completed

Hook-and-Ring Toy

Ring can be a bracelet. Fit it in your mom and dad's wrist and play a ring and hook game together!

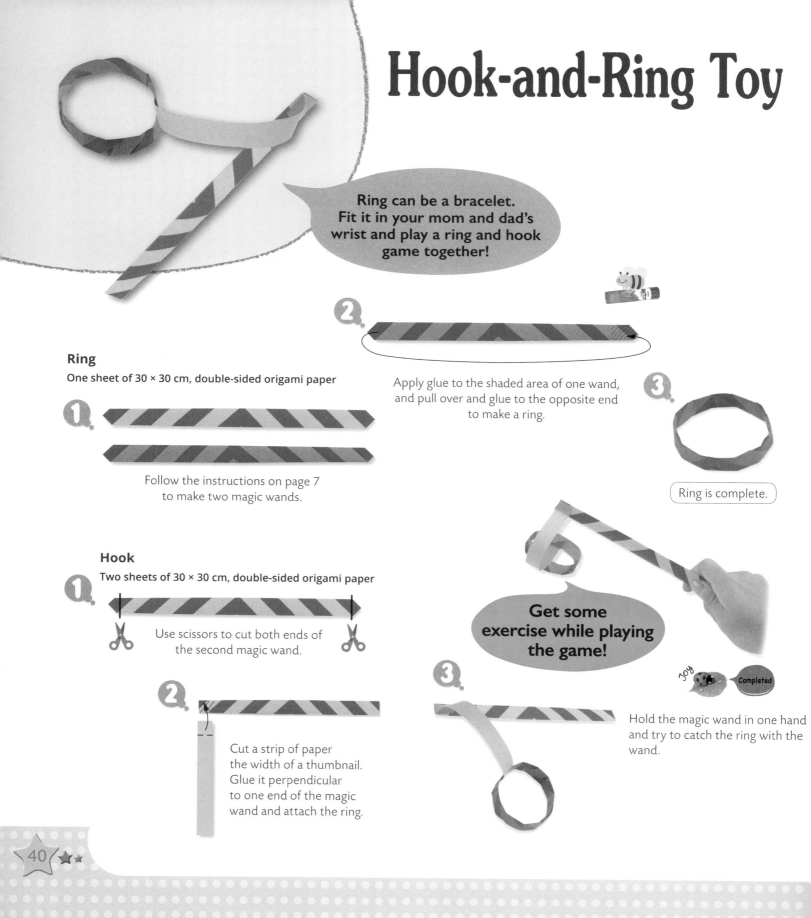

Ring

One sheet of 30 × 30 cm, double-sided origami paper

1. Follow the instructions on page 7 to make two magic wands.

2. Apply glue to the shaded area of one wand, and pull over and glue to the opposite end to make a ring.

3. Ring is complete.

Hook

Two sheets of 30 × 30 cm, double-sided origami paper

1. Use scissors to cut both ends of the second magic wand.

2. Cut a strip of paper the width of a thumbnail. Glue it perpendicular to one end of the magic wand and attach the ring.

3. Hold the magic wand in one hand and try to catch the ring with the wand.

Get some exercise while playing the game!

Completed

Cup-and-Ball Toy

Catch the ball in the cup! Play the game with your friends!

1. **Three sheets of 15 × 15 cm, double-sided origami paper**

Following the instructions on page 7, make a magic wand. Snip its ends, fold it in half, and attach each end to either side of the bottom of a cup.

2.

Magic wand attached to the cup.

3.

Make two more magic wands, and glue their ends together to make two loops. Insert one loop into another as shown, and staple a rubber band to the top.

4.

Staple the other end of the rubber band to the edge of the cup.

Joy   Completed

Chapter 2
Crowns

Wear a colorful crown and proclaim,
"I'll be the best in the world!"
Share your dreams and courage
with your friends!

What are your dreams?

I have practiced paper-folding my entire life.
I have come up with many models, among the most
popular of which are crowns. Once I demonstrate how
to make them and let my pupils put them on, everyone—from
children to grandparents—falls in love with them
and begins photographing them with their cellphones.
Sometimes I ask myself why everybody loves wearing crowns.
Children, I think, love them because they help them imagine
the kings, queens, princes, and princesses of fairy tales.
Adults, I think, wear them to forget their problems
and to imagine themselves as the best in their fields.
So let's make crowns and proclaim,
"My dream! I will achieve it.
I'll be the best in the world!
But you can achieve your dream too!"
Let's wear crowns and encourage
each other to be the best we can be!

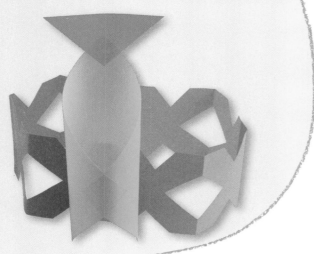

Jewel Crown

Don a jewel crown and play a character. Pretend you're the king, queen, prince, or princess that you want to be!

1. **Three sheets of 15 × 15 cm, double-sided origami paper**

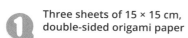

Layer two sheets and cut in half into four sheets.

2.

Layer four sheets and fold in half.

3.

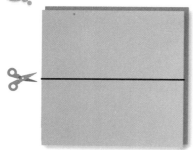

Cut along the lines as shown in the image, and unfold.

4.

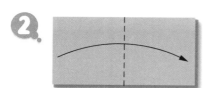

One by one, glue the four sheets into a circlet that is the right size for your head.

7.

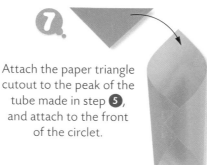

Attach the paper triangle cutout to the peak of the tube made in step **5**, and attach to the front of the circlet.

Joy *Completed*

6.

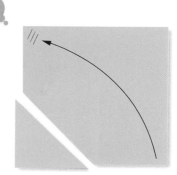

Apply glue to the shaded area and draw round to attach to the opposite corner.

5.

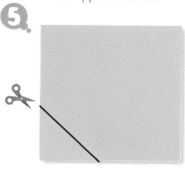

Cut the corner of the remaining sheet as shown in the image.

V Crown

This is a crown that means "Victory."
Place it on a friend's head and announce,
"You're the best!"

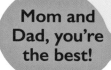

Mom and Dad, you're the best!

Three sheets of 15 × 15 cm, double-sided origami paper

1.

Fold in half.

2.

Fold in half again.

3.

Cut along the line as indicated in the image, and unfold.

4.

The "V" is complete.

5.

Layer two sheets and cut in half into four sheets.

6.

Layer these four sheets, and cut along the lines shown in the image.

Joy   Completed

7.

One by one, glue the four sheets into a circlet that is the right size for your head, and glue the "V" to the front.

★★ 45

Heart Crown

This is a crown with a lovely heart at its center.

Two sheets of 15 × 15 cm, double-sided origami paper

1. Layer two sheets and cut in half into four sheets.

2. Layer four sheets and fold in half.

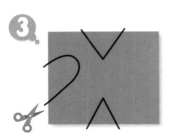

3. Cut the folded sheets along the lines shown in the image.

4.

Glue the shaded sections of each of the four sections and attach them to each other in a circlet.

Decorate the crown with the two cut-out hearts.

Prince Crown

Five or six sheets of 15 × 15 cm, double-sided origami paper

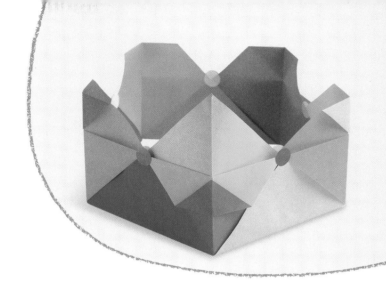

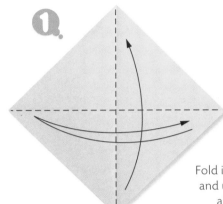

1. Fold in half along vertical axis and unfold, then fold in half along horizontal axis.

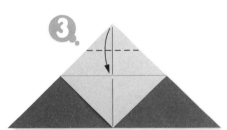

2. Fold only top layer down to base, as shown.

3. Fold the bottom layer down to the edge of the fold made in step **2**, as shown.

4. Repeat steps **1**-**3** on four or five additional sheets of origami paper.

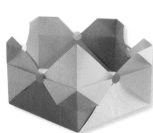

Decorate the crown with stickers.

Joy — Completed

I am a prince! What about you?

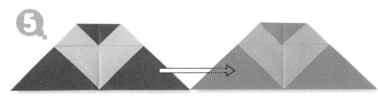

5. Glue two sheets side by side, as shown.

6. Glue the rest of the sheets together to form a crown the right size for your head.

Native American Crown

Wear the crown to play a Native American.

I am a Native American princess!

Crown

One sheet of A4 (21 × 29.7 cm) double-sided origami paper

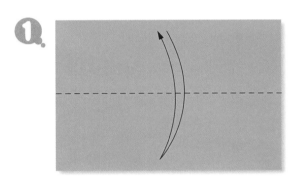

1. Fold in half and unfold.

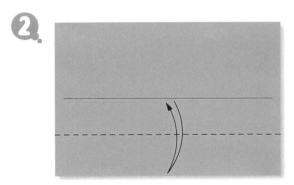

2. Fold bottom edge to central horizontal fold and unfold.

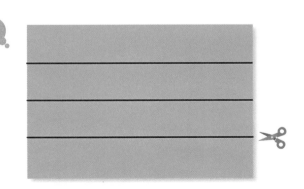

3. Cut into four equal parts as in the image.

Feather shaft

One sheet of 15 × 15 cm, double-sided origami paper

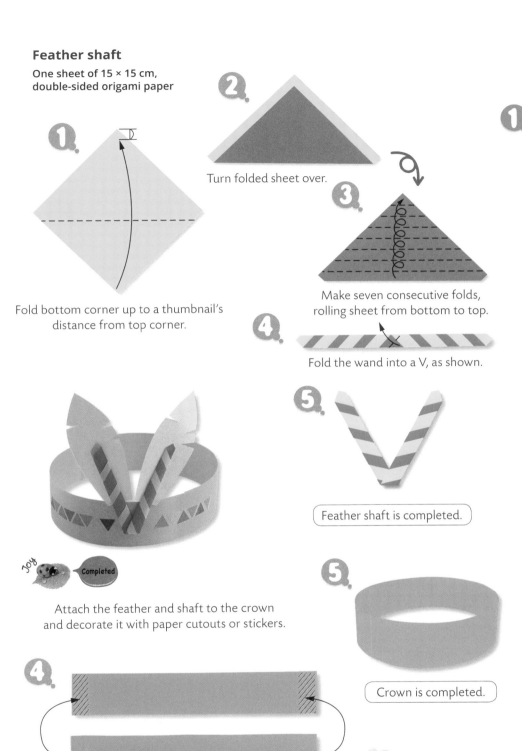

1. Fold bottom corner up to a thumbnail's distance from top corner.

2. Turn folded sheet over.

3. Make seven consecutive folds, rolling sheet from bottom to top.

4. Fold the wand into a V, as shown.

5. Feather shaft is completed.

Attach the feather and shaft to the crown and decorate it with paper cutouts or stickers.

Joy Completed

4. Apply glue to the shaded areas and attach the four pieces to each other to create a ring (see illustration to step **5**), making sure it's the right size for your head.

5. Crown is completed.

Feather

One sheet of 15 × 15 cm, single-sided origami paper

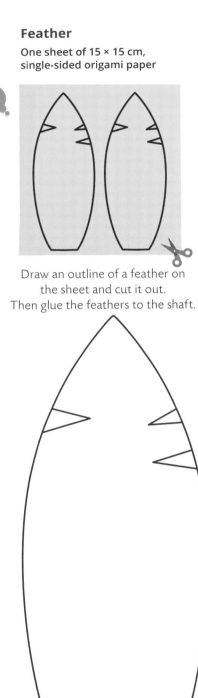

1. Draw an outline of a feather on the sheet and cut it out.
Then glue the feathers to the shaft.

Crown with Teddy Bear Face

 Crown

One sheet of A4 (21 × 29.7 cm),
double-sided origami paper

1.

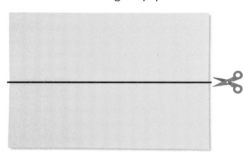

Fold sheet in half and cut along
crease.

2.

Fold each of the sheets in half
lengthwise, and unfold.

3.

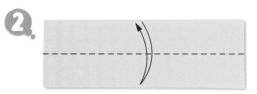

Cut along the lines as shown in the image.
Do this with both sheets.

6.

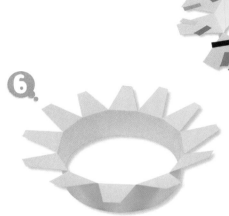

Fold the prongs outward and decorate as you wish.

5.

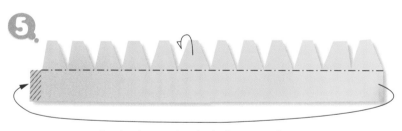

Apply glue to the shaded area, and join one
end to the other to make a crown.

4.

Apply glue to the shaded area,
and join the two sheets.

Attach the face of the
Teddy Bear to the crown.

Animal Face

One sheet of 15 × 15 cm, double-sided origami paper

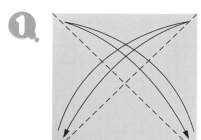

1. Fold along each diagonal and unfold as shown.

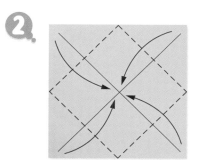

2. Fold each corner towards center, as shown.

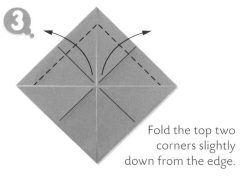

3. Fold the top two corners slightly down from the edge.

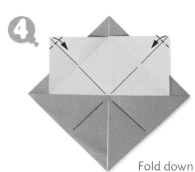

4. Fold down tips, as shown.

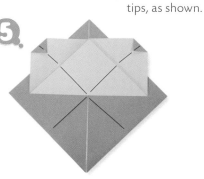

5. Turn model over.

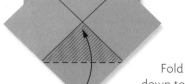

6. Fold the top corner down towards the rear. Apply glue to the shaded area, and fold up the bottom corner.

To make a lion, cut a 15 × 15 cm sheet of origami paper into the shape of a mane, and glue it to the back of the face.

Use eye stickers to create the face of a Teddy Bear.

Princess Crown and Peaked Hat

Use magic wands to make the crown,
then decorate the top with a peaked hat.

 Crown

Six sheets of 30 × 30 cm, double-sided origami paper

1.

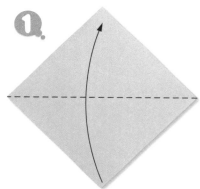

Fold two sheets in half.

Use glue for a decorative
peaked hat.

6.

Tape the
magic wands
at the center.

5.

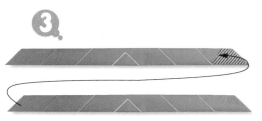

Follow the instructions on page 7 to make
4 magic wands. Arrange and attach
them to the circlet as shown.

2.

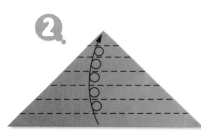

Working from the bottom up,
make six narrow folds,
as shown, in both sheets.

3.

Glue the two, as shown.

4.

Attach one end to the other
to create a circlet.

Peaked Hat

Two sheets of 15 × 15 cm, double-sided origami paper

 1.

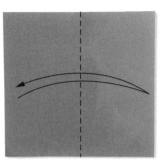

Fold in half and unfold.

2.

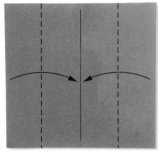

Fold each side to the centerline.

3.

Fold in half towards the rear.

4.

Fold both top corners down to the centerline.

5.

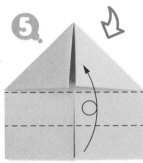

Make two consecutive folds from the bottom up with the top layer.

6.

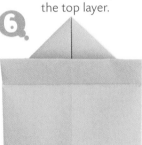

Turn model around.

7.

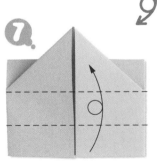

Make two consecutive folds from the bottom up on the other side.

8.

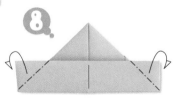

Fold the edges down as shown on the top only.

9.

Push the back from the front to make the hat three-dimensional.

Joy! Joy!

Joy Completed

The peaked hat is completed.

Make two and insert one into the other, as shown.

Like a Princess, you're the best in the world!

Duck Hat, Bow, and Flower

Wear a duck hat and sing "Old McDonald Had a Farm"!
The duck goes quack, quack! The cow goes moo, moo!

 **Duck Hat**

One sheet of 30 × 30 cm, double-sided origami paper
One sheet of 15 × 15 cm, double-sided origami paper

1.

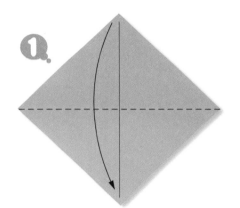

Fold the 30 × 30 cm sheet in half into a triangle, as shown.

2.

Fold left corner of the triangle down to the bottom corner. Flip the model over.

3.

Fold left corner down to the bottom corner, as shown.

4.

Fold the bottom corner up and behind and glue it to the inside of the sheet.

5.

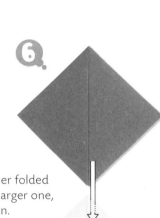

Follow the first four steps with the 15 × 15 cm sheet.

6.

Insert the smaller folded square into the larger one, as shown.

7.

Apply glue to the shaded area, fold down the upper half of the smaller square as shown.

Bow

Two sheets of 7.5 × 7.5 cm, double-sided origami paper

1. Fold sheet in half to create a triangle.

2. Fold triangle in half.

3. Do the same with the second sheet.

Joy · Completed

Arrange them corner to corner, as shown and place a sticker at the center.

8. Draw eyes or attach stickers to the duck to create eyes.

Flower

One sheet of 7.5 × 7.5 cm, double-sided origami paper

1. Fold square in half.

2. Fold in half again.

3. Draw edge of flower, as shown, and cut along line. Unfold.

Joy · Completed

Joy · Completed

Roosters go cock-a-doodle-doo! Geese go honk, honk!

Wow!

Chapter 3
Paper Cup Toys

We can use our imagination to see new things in common forms.
Discover ways of making things out of everyday objects!
Don't be afraid to experiment!

We gain new perspectives from the way in which we look at things.

I make lots of things out of empty milk cartons,
paper cups, wooden chopsticks, and straws.
I am constantly thinking about new ways of folding paper.
In the morning, I watch birds sing and re-create them out of paper.
I watch leaves flutter down and create pinwheels.
I hate throwing things away and think about
how to use them for paper-folding.
I draw on empty toilet paper rolls or
empty boxes and use them as backdrops for my creations.
One day, I saw some workers throwing away
paper cups after drinking their coffee, so
I used these for paper-folding projects as well.
Don't provide all the answers to our children;
rather, give them an opportunity to discover various
possibilities and perspectives.
Now, let's enter a new world
through paper cups and sheets of paper!

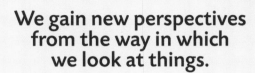

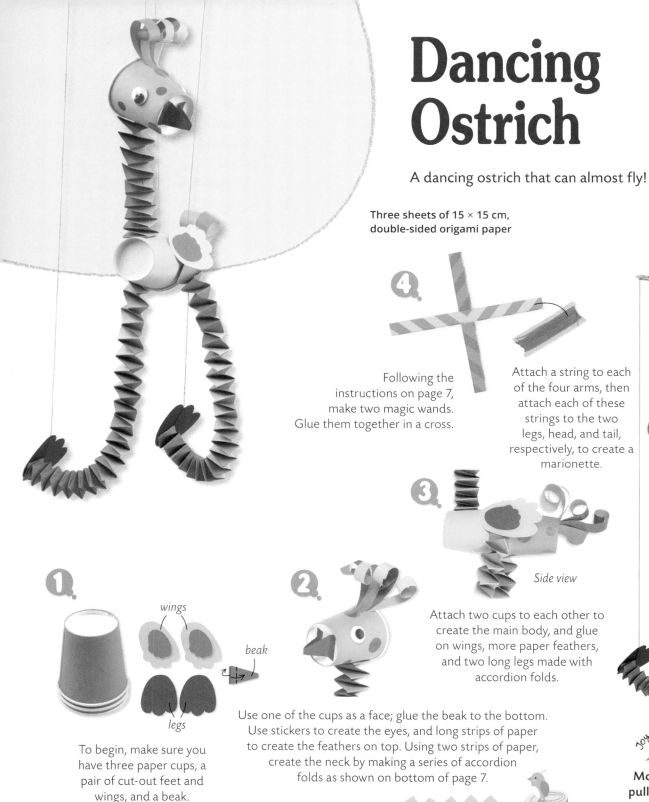

Dancing Ostrich

A dancing ostrich that can almost fly!

Three sheets of 15 × 15 cm, double-sided origami paper

4. Following the instructions on page 7, make two magic wands. Glue them together in a cross.

Attach a string to each of the four arms, then attach each of these strings to the two legs, head, and tail, respectively, to create a marionette.

3. *Side view*

Attach two cups to each other to create the main body, and glue on wings, more paper feathers, and two long legs made with accordion folds.

1.

wings

beak

legs

To begin, make sure you have three paper cups, a pair of cut-out feet and wings, and a beak.

2. Use one of the cups as a face; glue the beak to the bottom. Use stickers to create the eyes, and long strips of paper to create the feathers on top. Using two strips of paper, create the neck by making a series of accordion folds as shown on bottom of page 7.

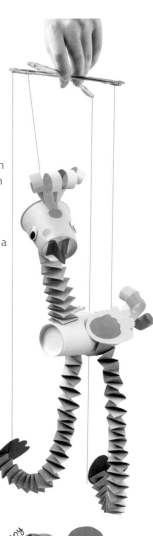

 Joy Completed

Move the ostrich by pulling on the strings.

Boomerang Octopus and Windmill

Grab the octopus by one of its tentacles and fling it in the air. It will spin while flying!

 ## Boomerang Octopus

Four sheets of 15 × 15 cm, double-sided origami paper

1.

Make four magic wands, following directions on page 7. Glue them to each other as shown, and attach stickers to their ends.

2.

Attach stickers to the cup to create a face, then glue the wands to its bottom.

 ## Windmill

Three sheets of 15 × 15 cm, double-sided origami paper

1.

Make three magic wands (see page 7). Glue together as shown to create the blades of the windmill. Then decorate an empty milk carton to resemble a windmill, make a hole on facings sides of the carton, and stick the straw through it.

Let's make the windmill spin!

Turn the blades by turning the straw from behind.

Smiling Puppets, 1 and 2

Grab the back of the cup by hand and open and shut it to make the puppet laugh or speak.

Two sheets of 15 × 15 cm, double-sided origami paper

1.

Fold in half.

2.

Cut strips along one end of the folded sheet, as shown (the puppet's hair).

3.

Cut a long slit on either side of a paper cup.

4.

Unfold.

Let's all smile! Smiling makes us happy!

Joy Completed

Decorate the face and the body in diverse ways.

6.

Cut out the shape of hands, shoes, lips, etc. and attach to complete body.

5.

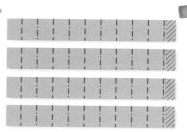

Make a series of accordion folds in four long strips of paper. Apply glue to the shaded areas, and attach these to the paper cup to make arms and legs.

Deer and Dog House

Rudolph the Red-Nosed Reindeer had a very shiny nose! Move his body to move his head!

One sheet of 20 × 15 cm, double-sided origami paper
One sheet of 5 × 5 cm, double-sided origami paper

1.

Fold the 20 × 15 cm sheet in half and cut along the lines to create body and legs.

2.

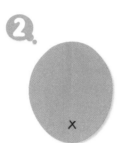

Cut the belly out of the 5 × 5 sheet.

3.

Draw some antlers on the scraps of the 20 × 15 sheet and cut them out.

4.

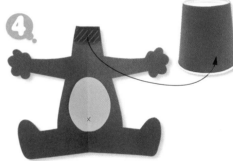

Apply glue to the shaded area on the neck, and attach the cup, as shown.

Decorate the face as you wish.

Dog House

Roof
One sheet of 16 × 15 cm, double-sided origami paper

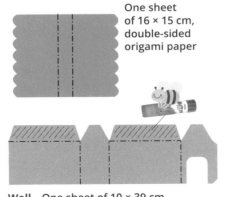

Wall   One sheet of 10 × 39 cm, double-sided origami paper

Talking Puppet

Grab the magic wands and move them up and down to open and shut the puppet's mouth! Make your puppet speak to your friends.

Two sheets of 15 × 15 cm, double-sided origami paper
Two sheets of 5 × 5 cm, double-sided origami paper
Two paper cups

Speak politely! Speak clearly and intelligently to say whatever you wish to say!

1. Following the instructions on page 7, make two magic wands, and snip their edges.

2. Glue the wands to the two cups as shown.

3.
5 cm
5 cm
Place two 5 × 5 cm sheets on top of each other, draw a hand on the top one, and cut it out.

15 cm
2 cm
To make arms, cut out two 15 × 2 cm strips and make a series of accordion folds in them.

4. Glue hands to arms, and glue arms to cup. Create the face out of stickers or paper cut-outs.

Joy   Completed

Move the wands to open and close the mouth.

Exercising Puppet

Friends! Let's exercise together to strengthen our friendship!

Be careful when using a cutter!

1.

Using scissors and a cutter, cut strips in the cup as shown.

2.

Cut a 21 × 4 cm strip, and punch a hole at one end, as shown.

3.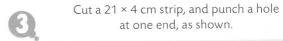

Cut two 12 × 2.5 cm strips, and punch a hole at one end, as shown.

Have some stickers and plastic pins on hand.

One! two! three! four!

Push the strip at the bottom up and down to make the arms move.

 Joy Completed

5.

Slip the cup over the head of the puppet, as shown.

4.

Pin the three strips of paper together with the plastic pin, and decorate the hands and face.

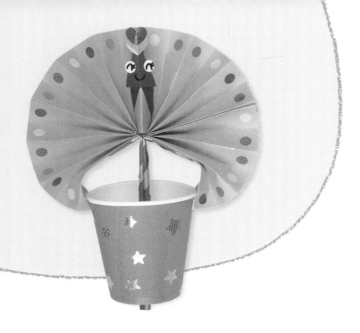

Hide-and-Seek Peacock

Hold the cup while pulling the stick down.
The peacock will unfold its wings
and disappear inside the cup!

Face

One sheet of 15 × 15 cm, double-sided origami paper

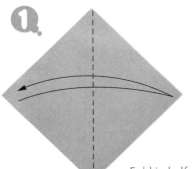

1. Fold in half and unfold.

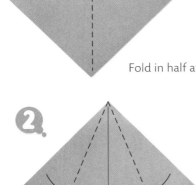

2. Fold sides down along the centerline.

Model after fold.

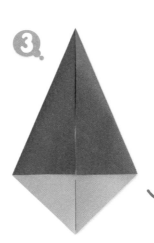

3.

4. Fold up the bottom corner as shown.

The head is completed.

Create the face from stickers.

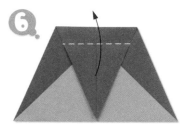

6. Fold the tip back up, creating a new fold slightly below the upper edge, as shown.

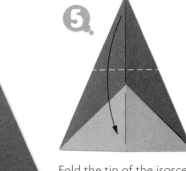

5. Fold the tip of the isosceles triangle down to the bottom edge.

Wings

Four sheets of 15 × 15 cm, double-sided origami paper

1.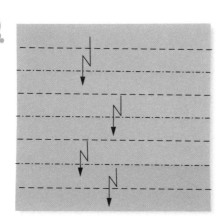

Fold the sheet with a series of accordion folds from top to bottom.

2.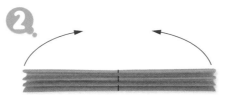

Fold the accordion in half, as shown.

3.

Apply glue to the inside of the fold and press the two sides together to create a fan.

4.

Repeat steps **1**-**3** with another sheet of paper, and glue the two fans together to create the wings.

5.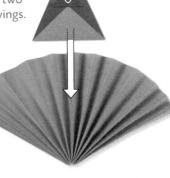

Insert the head into the joined wings and glue it securely.

6.

Following the instructions on page 7, make two magic wands. Glue them to the sides of the wings, and to each other at the base.

Seek!   Hide!

Joy   Completed

Make a hole in the cup and pass the wand through the cup.

Friends, when you see grown-ups, make sure to greet them with a polite "hello"!

Waving Puppet 1 and 2

Move the straw up and down to make the puppet say "hello" while moving its arms!

One sheet of 15 × 15 cm, double-sided origami paper

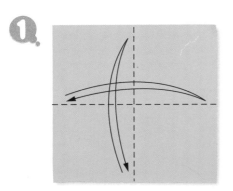

1. Fold and unfold to make a crease.

2. Fold top edge down to central crease.

3. Flip model over and fold bottom up to crease.

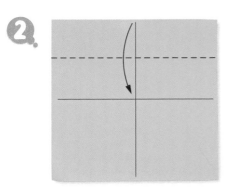

Make the waving puppet by following the image.

Joy — Completed

4. Fold both sides inwards, towards crease.

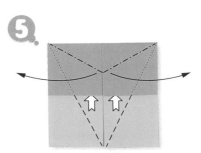

5. Grab the inside in the direction of the arrow and fold.

6. Reverse-fold.

7. Turn model over and fold along the line, as shown.

8. Turn model over and fold the edges, as shown.

9. Back of head after all folds are made.

10. Front of head, after all folds are made.

The face is completed.

Hello!

The puppet waves "hello" when the straws are moved up and down.

12. Cut the hands and bow out of a sheet of paper and glue them on the figure as shown.

11. Punch holes in the cup, and pass the straws through.

How are you? It's nice to meet you!

Joy

Completed

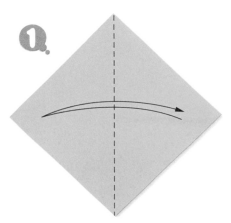

Bobble-Head Goblin

Move the straw and the goblin will move its face right and left!

One sheet of 15 × 15 cm, double-sided origami paper

1.

Fold and unfold the sheet to make a crease.

2.

Fold outer edges to the central crease.

3.

Fold bottom corner up to create a triangle.

4.

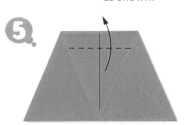

Fold the top corner down to the bottom edge, as shown.

5.

Fold this same corner up again, slightly below the top edge, as shown.

6.

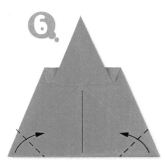

Fold both bottom corners in, as shown.

7.

Flip the model over.

8.

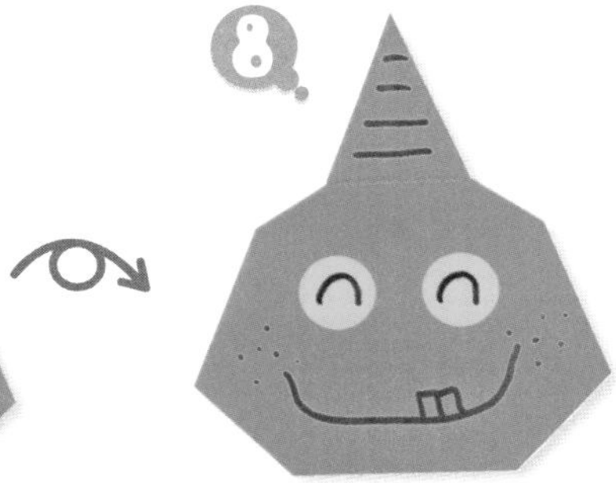

The head is finished. Draw eyes and a mouth, or decorate with stickers.

9.

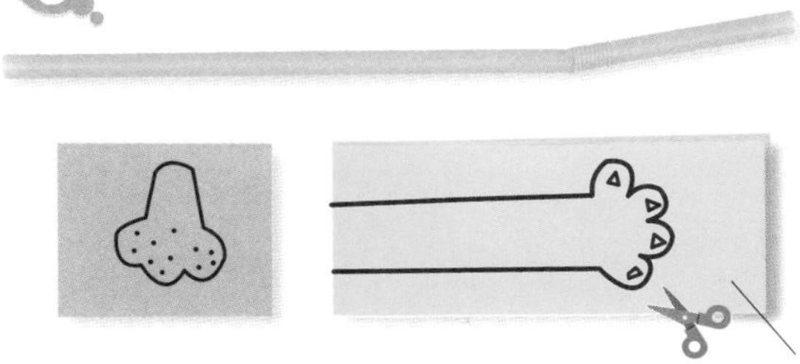

Draw and cut out a nose. Layer one sheet of paper over another; draw and cut out the arms.

Overlap two sheets.

10.

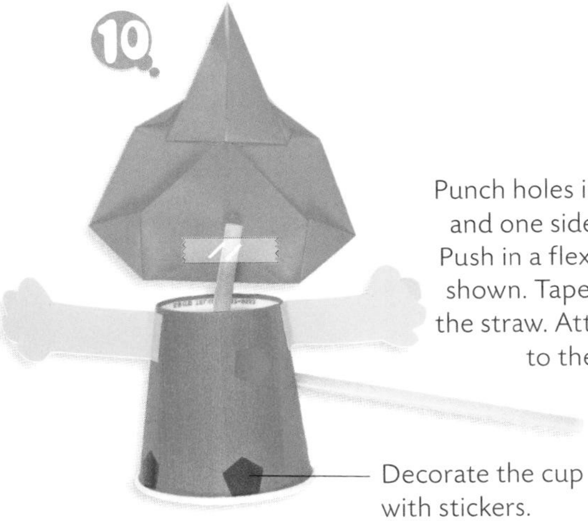

Punch holes in the bottom and one side of the cup. Push in a flexible straw, as shown. Tape the head to the straw. Attach the arms to the cup.

Decorate the cup with stickers.

Joy   Completed

Bobbling head! Bobbling head!

Flower Mobile

Use your favorite colors for the flowers and hang the mobile in the window. The breeze will make the flowers spin!

1 Nine sheets of 7.5 × 7.5 cm, double-sided origami paper

Draw the outlines of flowers on the paper and cut them out.

2

Attach the flowers with round stickers to a 60 cm piece of string.

Oh, yeah!

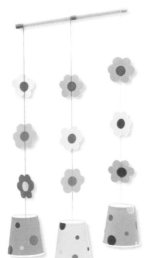

Wow!

4

3

Decorate the cup with stickers. Attach the string to the bottom of the cup with a piece of tape.

Make three of these, and tie them to a long stick.

Lovely Flowers

Six sheets of 7.5 × 7.5 cm, double-sided origami paper

1.
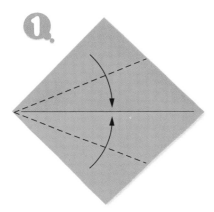
Fold both sides towards the center.

2.
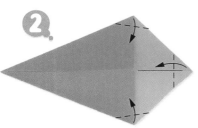
Fold three corners, as shown.

3.

Flip the model over.

4.

Repeat to make five more petals.

5.

Cut a small circle out of paper. Glue the petals to the circle, side by side.

6.

Turn the flower around and glue another round paper circle to the other side.

Attach desired number of petals to create a unique flower!

Wow, it's a beautiful flower!

Completed

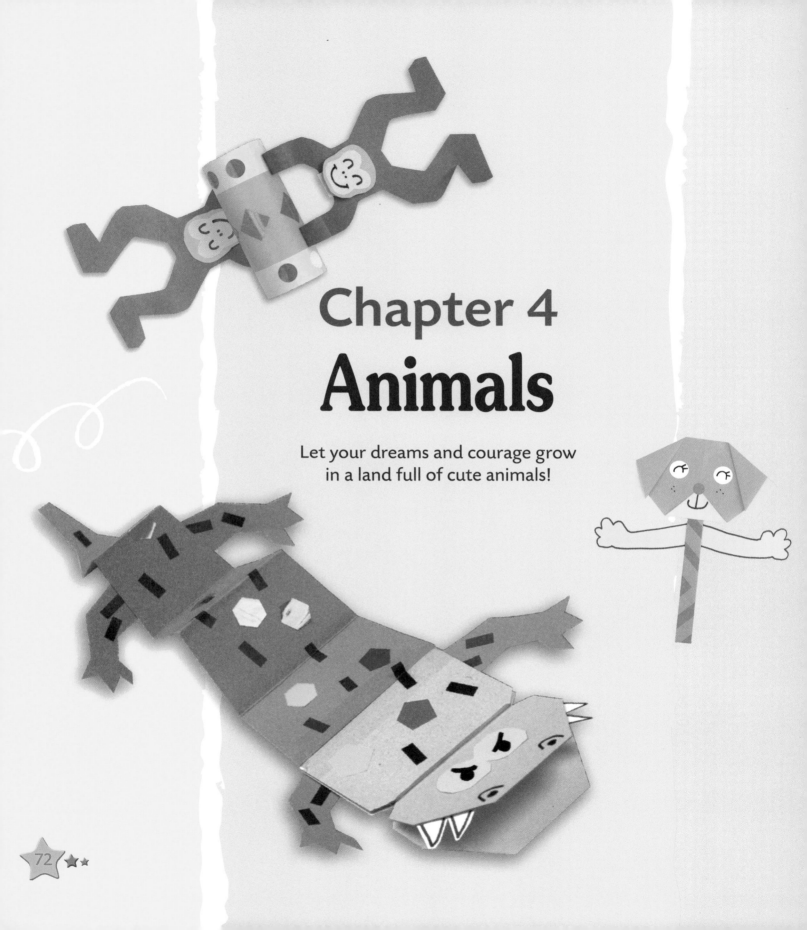

Chapter 4
Animals

Let your dreams and courage grow
in a land full of cute animals!

Let's enter the world of fairy tales!

While working on TV, I watched many programs
about depressed Millennials.
I don't understand how young people
can give up on so many things.
Youth is about challenges and having a fresh perspective.
Watching people give up on their dreams
made me feel sorry and sad.
Look at me. I became an expert in paper folding
by working at it all the time.
Paper folding can help you retain
your childhood curiosity, sense of wonder
and innocence as you mature into strong individuals
who never lose sight of their potential.
Now, let's move on to the world of adorable animals!

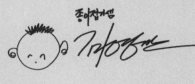

Elephant with Moving Trunk

Grab the elephant's rump to make his trunk move!

The trunk works like a hand. It can grab bananas!

One sheet of 15 × 15 cm, double-sided origami paper
Two sheets of 7.5 × 7.5 cm, single-sided origami paper

1.
Fold the sheet in half.

2.
Follow the image to draw an elephant on the folded sheet.

3.
The body of the elephant is complete.

I want to ride the elephant!

4.

Layering one sheet over another, draw a tusk and an ear and cut them out.

5.

Attach stickers to create the eyes and glue on the tusks and ears.

Grab and shake the elephant by its rear to make the nose move.

Joy Completed

Me too!

Joy!

Yes! Yes!

Nodding Elephant

A cute elephant that nods his head.
Whenever your friends say something,
use the elephant to reply: " Yes, that's right!"
and make it nod. Your friend will love it.

Face

One 15 × 15 cm sheet of double-sided origami paper

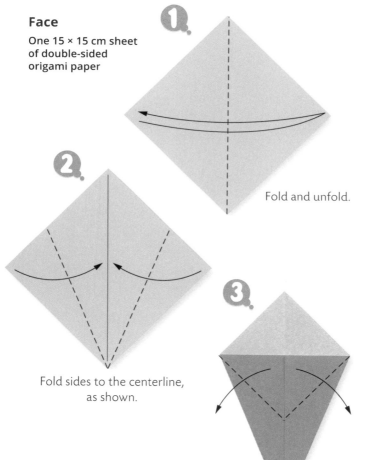

1. Fold and unfold.

2. Fold sides to the centerline, as shown.

3. Fold both sides down and away from the centerline.

4. Fold the upper tip down, as shown.

5. Fold the bottom tip towards the rear.

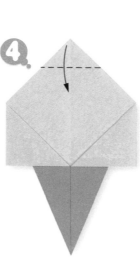

6. Flip the model over, and fold the corner 1/3 of the way down.

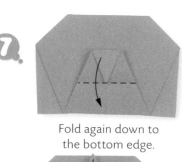

7. Fold again down to the bottom edge.

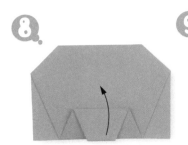

8. Unfold.

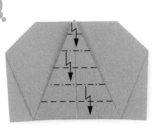

9. Make six accordion folds.

10. Draw in eyes and use stickers to decorate.

The face is completed.

Body
One sheet of 16 × 15 cm embossed origami paper

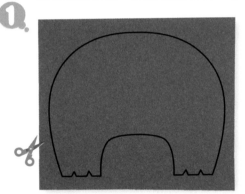

1. Draw the body on the sheet and cut it out.

The face will move when the wooden chopsticks are moved.

Joy Completed

2. Tie together two wooden chopsticks with a rubber band, as shown.

3. Tape the body to the wooden chopsticks, as shown, and tape the head to the end of the upright chopstick.

★★ 77

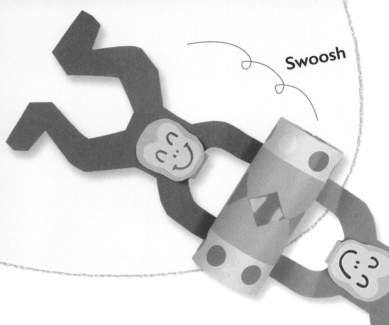

Swoosh

Playful Monkeys

Swoosh! Two monkeys are having fun rolling a tube. Let's have fun and play with them too!

Roll the tube and the weight of the battery inside will make the monkeys flip!

Tube
Two sheets of 15 × 15 cm, double-sided origami paper

1.

Cover an empty roll of toilet paper with one sheet of the paper and glue it in place.

2.

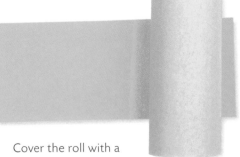

Cover the roll with a second, narrower sheet of paper, and glue it in place sheet to create a stripe at the bottom and top.

3.

The tube covered with both sheets.

4.

The tube is finished.

Decorate the tube with different kinds of stickers.

3. Attach the monkeys to the tube, as shown. Glue a used battery to the inside of the tube.

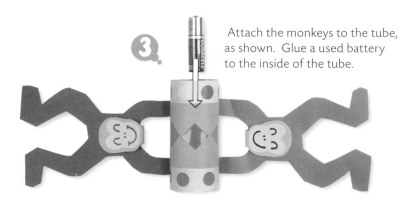

4. Have fun rolling the tube.

2. Fold the head down. On another small piece of paper, draw a face, cut it out, and glue it on the head.

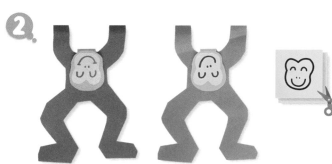

The monkey is completed.

Monkey

Two sheets of 15 × 15 cm, double-sided origami paper

1.

Place one sheet on top of the other; draw a monkey and cut it out.

I can do a flip too!

Crawling Crocodile

Hold the bottom jaw with one hand, and grab the crocodile's teeth with the other and pull them up and down to make the mouth open and close.

1.

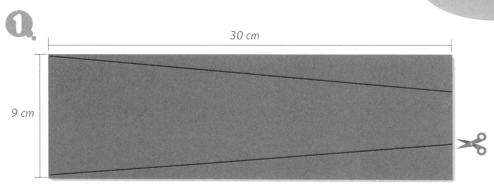

Take a 30 × 9 cm sheet of embossed paper and cut it as shown.

2.

Make five folds and cut the tail as shown.

3.

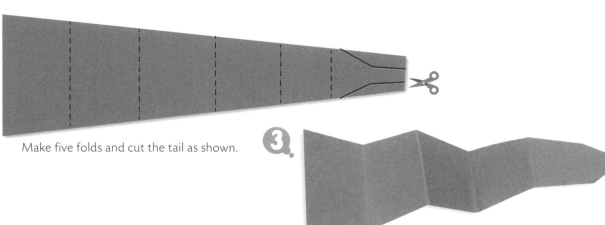

The body is completed.

6. Use tape to attach the jaws and feet to the body.

7. Stretch a rubber band over the jaws as shown in the photo, and decorate them with stickers. Now the crocodile can yawn.

5.

9 cm

5 cm

Draw and cut four legs out of 9 × 5 cm sheets of paper.

Draw the face and attach some teeth.

4.

11 cm

9 cm

Draw and cut the upper and lower jaws out of a 11 × 9 cm sheet of paper.

The crocodile is completed.

Joy Completed

Leaping Frog

Create a frog and see how far you can make it jump with your friends or family!

Press down then release the frog's rear end. It will leap quite far.

1. One sheet of 30 × 8 cm embossed origami paper

Fold in half.

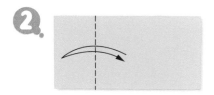

2.

Make a fold ¼ of the distance from the edge, and unfold.

4.

Folded sheet.

Profile view of accordion folds.

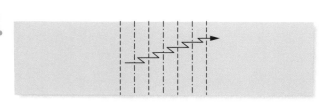

3.

Make a series of accordion folds in the center.

Jump! Jump!

5.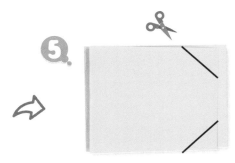

Cut off the corners on one side of the folded sheet, as shown.

6.

Model after cutting corners.

7.

Draw two eyes and four feet on yellow and green embossed paper; cut them out and glue to the body.

Completed

Cute Puppy 1 and 2

The puppy is barking! Use different types of eye stickers to create a variety of expressions.

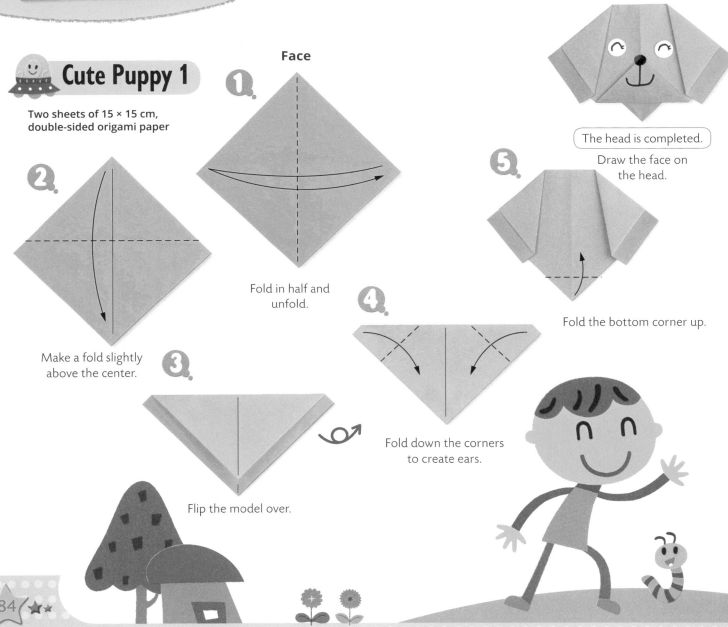

Cute Puppy 1

Two sheets of 15 × 15 cm, double-sided origami paper

Face

1. Fold in half and unfold.

2. Make a fold slightly above the center.

3. Flip the model over.

4. Fold down the corners to create ears.

5. Fold the bottom corner up.

The head is completed.

Draw the face on the head.

84 ★★★

Body

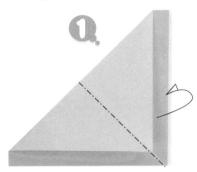

Follow steps **1**-**3** for head. Then fold in half towards the rear, as shown.

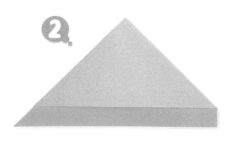

Body is completed.

Attach the face to the body.

Completed

Repeat steps **1**-**5** on page 84 to make a second head.

 **Cute Puppy 2**

Two sheets of 10 × 4 cm, double-sided origami paper

Lay one sheet on top of the other; draw an arm and cut it out.

Completed

Following the instructions on page 7, make a magic wand. Attach a puppy's head (following the instructions on the preceding page) to the wand, and glue on the arms.

Give me a name so you can call me!

How cute!

Cheep!
Cheep!

Chirping Chick

Fold both wings back, then release them.
The beak will move and make it seem as though the chick is chirping: "Cheep! Cheep!"

Two sheets of 15 × 15 cm, double-sided origami paper

1.
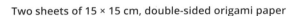
Lay one sheet on top of the other and fold in half.

2.
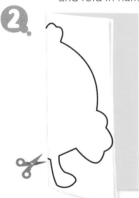
Draw the outline of a chick and cut it out.

3.

Separate one chick from the other.

4.
Fold one chick in half.

5.
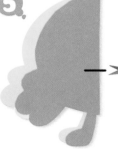
Make a short slit to create the chick's beak.

6.

Fold and unfold the top and bottom of the slit as shown.

Cluck
Cluck

Glue one half of the second chick cut-out to the rear of the first.

Do the same with the second half.

Grab the wings on either side, and fold and unfold the chick to make its beak move up and down.

Draw eyes on the chick's face.

The chick after the rear has been glued in place.

Cheep!

Cheep!

Cluck!

Running Centipede

Tie a rubber band to the front of the centipede and pull it along. Its legs will run.

Nine sheets of 15 × 15 cm of origami paper in different color

1.

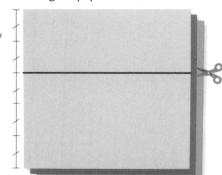

Layer three sheets on top of each other, and cut along the line, slightly above center as shown.

2.

Roll up the wider and narrower strips of paper and glue down the end to form cylinders.

6.

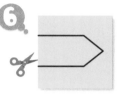

Draw and cut the tail out of a sheet of paper.

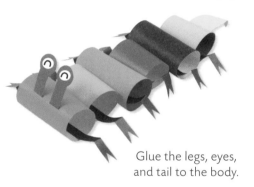

Glue the legs, eyes, and tail to the body.

5.

Lay two sheets of red paper, draw eyes as shown, and fold the bottom slightly as shown.

4.

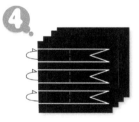

Layer four sheets of black paper. Draw three legs on them and cut these out.

3.

Glue the six cylinders to each other.

Dancing Octopus

After you make the octopus, pick it up and bounce it up and down. Its legs will start dancing!

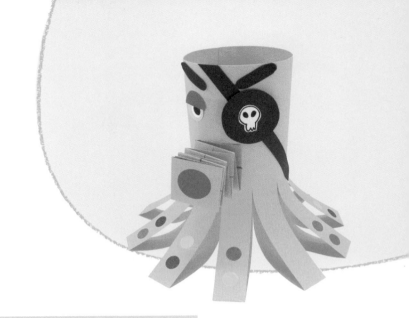

One sheet of 15 × 15 cm, double-sided origami paper

 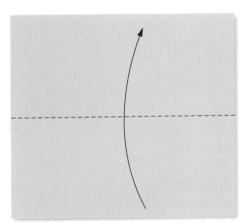

Fold in half from bottom to top.

Snip strips into the folded edge.

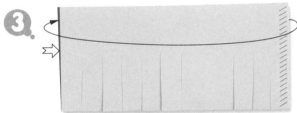

Apply glue to one edge, then pull the sheet around and insert the glued edge inside the edge on the opposite side. Hold until the glue sets.

Paste the nose on the octopus and decorate his face.

Make a series of accordion folds in a narrow strip of paper (see instructions on page 7) to create the nose.

Grab the octopus and press down to pick up light objects.

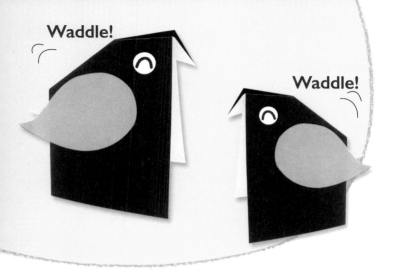

Waddle!

Waddle!

Waddling Penguin

Place the penguins on a hard surface and make it waddle by pushing it side to side.

1. Two sheets of 15 × 15 cm, double-sided origami paper

Fold in half along the diagonal.

2.

Fold corner inward.

3.

Make an inverse fold and push corner inside.

4.

Use a sticker for an eye.

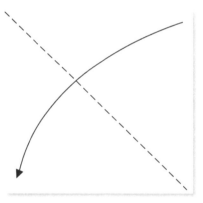

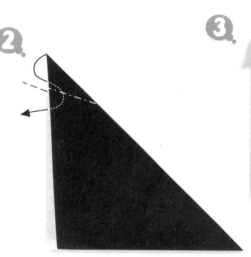

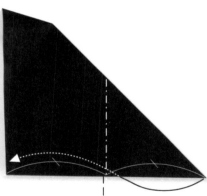

Two sheets of 7.5 × 7.5 cm, double-sided origami paper

5. Place one sheep over the other, draw a wing and cut it out.

6. Glue a wing to both sides of the penguin's body.

Joy   Completed

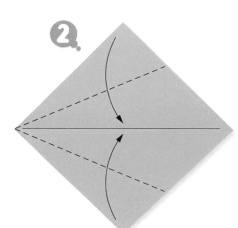

Nod! Nod!

Eating Duck

Paper folding is an art.
The act of folding simple paper, combining colors, and hearing the sound of folding stimulates the senses of children and helps them develop patience.

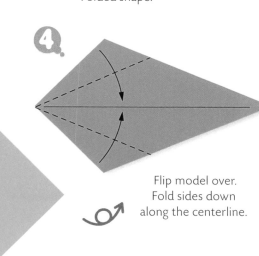

6.

Fold corner in at the line, as shown.

One sheet of 15 × 15 cm, double-sided origami paper

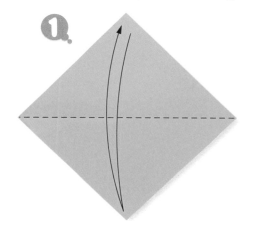

1.

Fold in half and unfold.

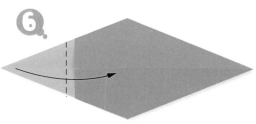

5.

Folded shape.

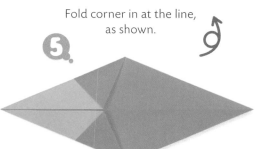

4.

Flip model over.
Fold sides down along the centerline.

2.

Fold along the centerline.

3.

Folded shape.

7.

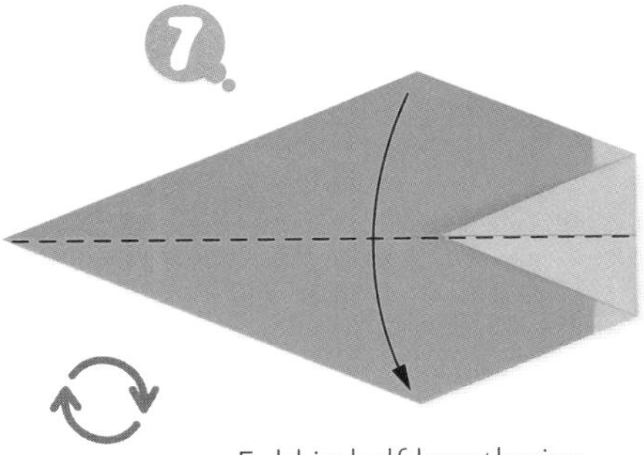

Fold in half lengthwise.

8.

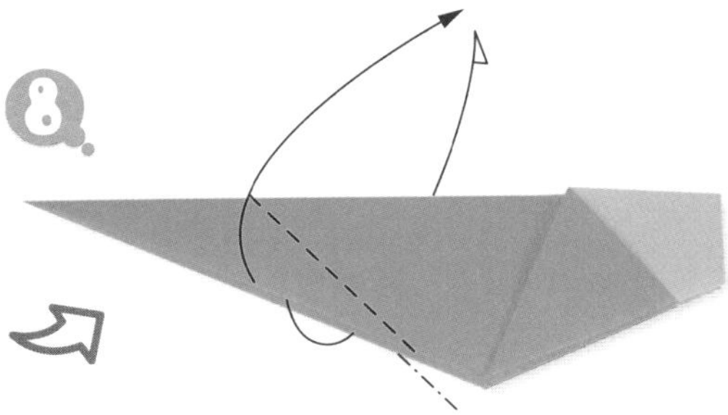

Make a reverse fold.

9.

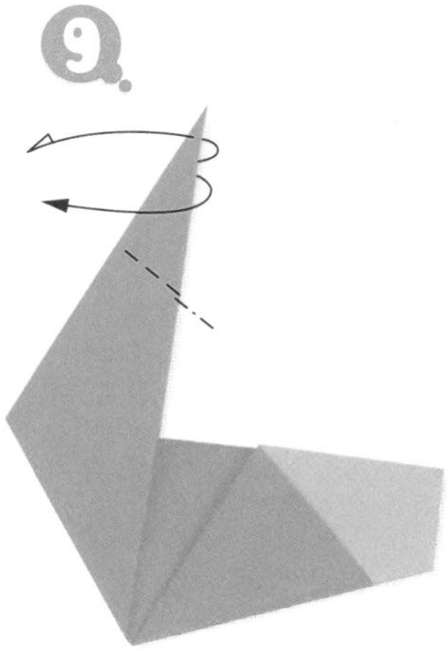

Make another reverse fold, as shown.

Joy

Completed

11.

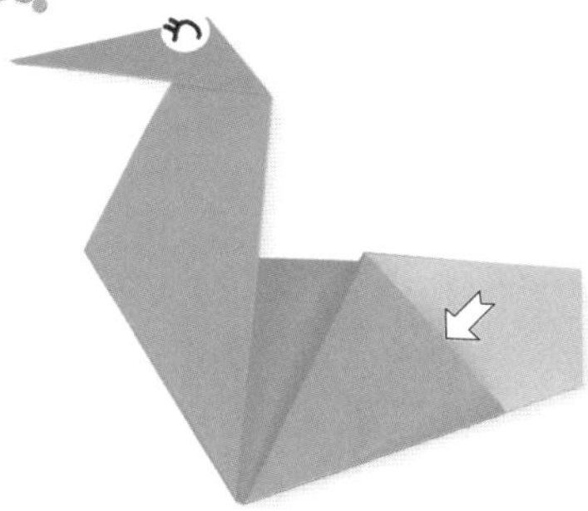

Insert finger into side pocket to add dimension.

10.

Use eye stickers for the eyes.

Insert your thumb and index finger into to the folds of the duck's rear and open and close them. The duck will look as though it is feeding.

Bird Purse

Hang the bird purse from your shoulder
when you go to a picnic.
You can also design other animal purses!

One sheet of 30 × 30 cm, double-sided origami paper
Four sheets of 15 × 15 cm, single-sided origami paper

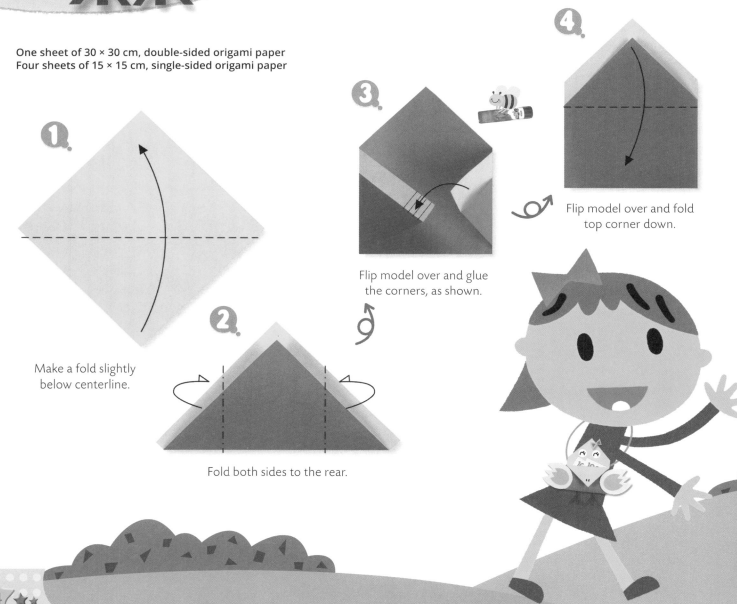

1. Make a fold slightly
below centerline.

2. Fold both sides to the rear.

3. Flip model over and glue
the corners, as shown.

4. Flip model over and fold
top corner down.

6.

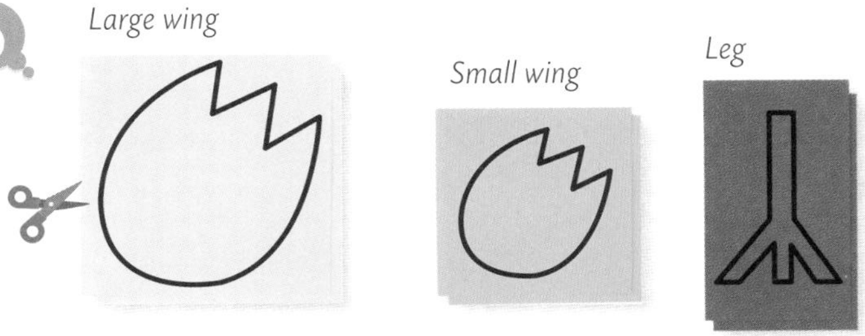

Large wing

Small wing

Leg

Layer one sheet on top of another for each body part. Draw both wings and legs, and cut them out.

5.

7.

Glue small wings onto large wings. Attach a wing to each side of bird's body. Draw in a face and decorate with a bow.

Joy Completed

Make play money and stick it into your wallet to play a game at the fair. It'll be fun, won't it?

Dinosaur

Make a fantastic dinosaur, a popular animal among children, and enjoy paper folding!

I am dinosaur conquering the Earth in the ancient past! I am a friend of stegosaurus and tyrannosaurus!

One sheet of 15 × 15 cm, double-sided origami paper

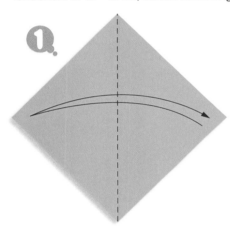

Fold in half and unfold.

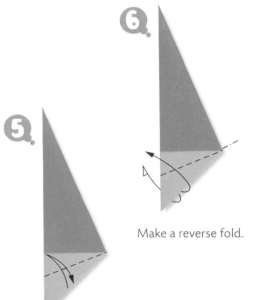

Fold along the angle shown, and unfold.

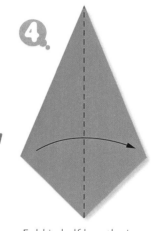

Make a reverse fold.

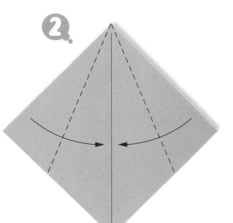

Fold sides towards the centerline.

(Folded model)

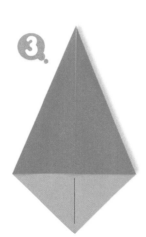

Fold in half lengthwise.

7. Fold and unfold at the angle shown.

8. Make an inside reverse fold.

9. Make another inside reverse fold to create the head.

10. Fold inside.

11. Fold in steps.

12. Push the sides out to add dimension.

I come from the mysterious world of the dinosaurs! My friends, shall we go look for the long-lost secrets of the dinosaurs.

Joy Completed

Chapter 5
Moving Toys

Whenever you encounter something difficult
or impossible to do, just say,
"It's so easy!"

It depends on your mindset. It's so easy!

When I'm on TV, I often say: "It's so easy!"
Of course, not everything we do is easy.
In fact, I too have experienced
adversity and ordeals in my life.
But when I encounter them,
I say to myself, "It's so easy!"
Positive thinking has enabled me to overcome
difficult things and make everything better.
When we think of something as impossible,
it makes it more difficult to do. Relax your mind
and play with sheets of paper for fun.
There are many things you can create simply with sheets
of paper and no special tools.
You can feel a sense of accomplishment even by
creating simple things out of paper.
Enhance your confidence and willingness
to tackle new challenges!

Swoosh!

Moving Alien

Swoosh! An alien just escaped from a spacecraft!

One sheet of 15 × 15 cm, double-sided origami paper

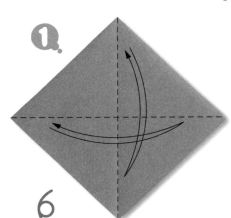

1. Fold in half from corner to corner and unfold.

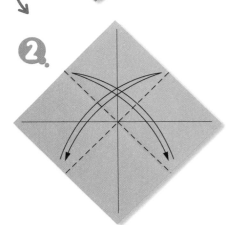

2. Flip model over; fold and unfold, as shown.

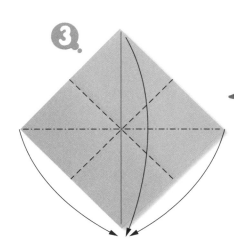

3. Gather and fold (square-pocket folding).

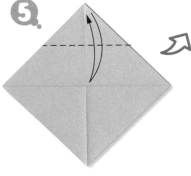

5. Fold only the upper side and unfold along the centerline.

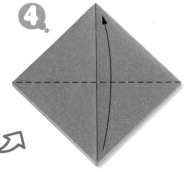

4. A square pocket is completed.

Fold only the front side in half.

100 ★★

6. Fold the upper side only in steps.

7. Fold down. Do it one more time on the reverse side. (step **4** to step **7**).

8. Cut along the line, as shown.

9. Attach stickers to create eyes on the triangle, and insert it into the bottom again.

10. Grab the two corners with the dots sections with both hands and rub them up and down. The triangle-face will go up.

Joy   Completed

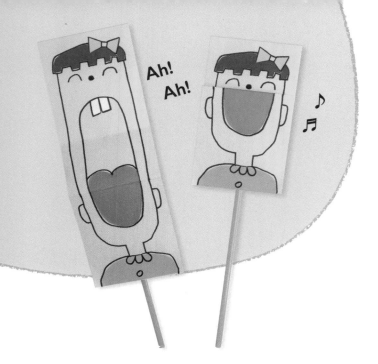

Singing Faces

Open your mouth and sing out loud. Let's listen to our friends and see which of them open their mouths the most and sing best!

One sheet of 10 × 30 cm, double-sided origami paper

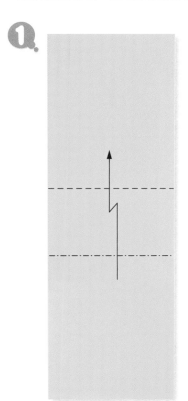

1.

Make two folds as shown.

2.

(Folded model).

3.

Draw face smiling on the folded sheet.

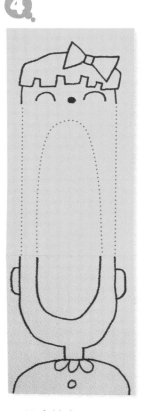

4.

Unfold the paper, and draw the rest of the face.

5. After completing your drawing, refold the sheet as in step **2**.

6. Tape the end of a straw to the back of the upper portion of the sheet.

Attach a strip of paper to the lower portion of the sheet, and push the straw through it, as shown.

Paint in the drawing, as shown.

Joy Completed

Peekaboo!

Hide-and-Seek Clown

Pull on the round sticker and the clown will disappear!

The face is completed.

Draw a face on the head.

Face
One sheet of 15 × 15 cm, double-sided origami paper

1.

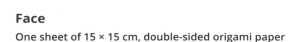

Fold in half and unfold.

2.

Fold sides down along the centerline.

3.

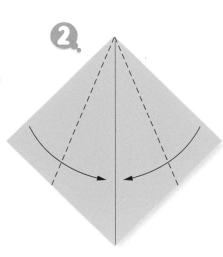

Fold both sides up,
as shown.

4.

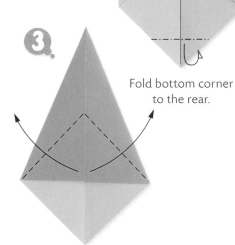

Fold bottom corner
to the rear.

Body

One sheet of 15 × 15 cm, double-sided origami paper and envelope

1.

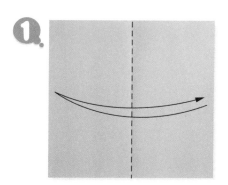

Fold and unfold.

2.

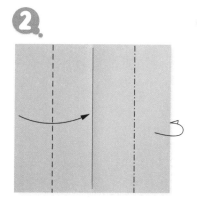

Fold each side to the central fold.

3.

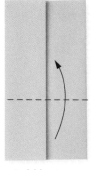

Fold bottom about 2/5 of the way up, as shown.

4.

Model after folding.

5.

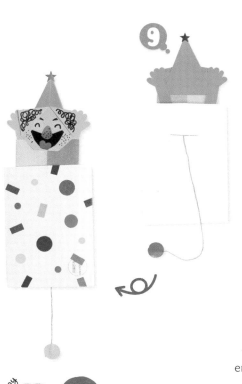

Attach face and arms to the body (to make the arms, see page 69).

7.

Cut the envelope as shown.

6.

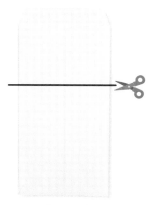

Tape a coin to a thread. Tape the coin to the back of the clown, and attach a sticker to the end of the thread.

9.

8.

Cut a horizontal slit towards the top of the envelope. Stick the clown into the envelope and pass the thread with the sticker through the slit in the back.

Joy   Completed

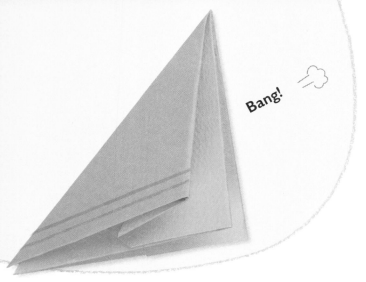

Bang!

Popgun

The sound of a popgun is loud even as it is made of newpaper!

One 27 × 39 cm, double-sided sheet of origami paper or newspaper

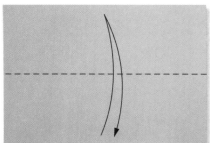

Fold sheet in half from top to bottom, and unfold.

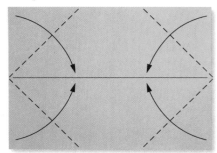

Fold all four corners down to the centerline.

Swing the folded model down, as shown and it will make a sharp popping sound.

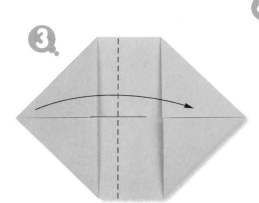

Fold model in half, as shown.

Joy Completed

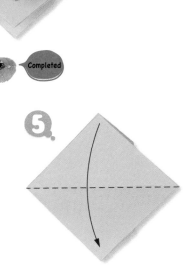

Fold in half from top to bottom.

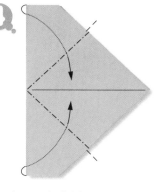

Make inside folds, as shown.

Flower Pinwheel

A slight breeze will make the pinwheel spin.

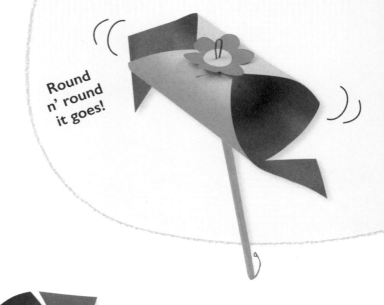

Round n' round it goes!

One sheet of 15 × 15 cm, double-sided origami paper

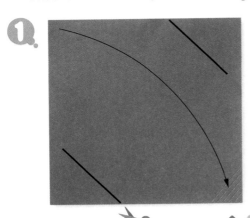

1. Cut along the line as shown, apply glue to the shaded area, and attach it to the opposite corner to create a tube.

2. Cut slits in the "wings" of the pinwheel, as shown.

3. Draw a flower on a 7.5. × 7.5 cm sheet of single-sided origami paper and cut it out.

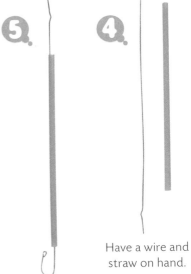

4. Have a wire and straw on hand.

5. Insert the wire into the straw, and bend up the end of the wire.

6. Attach the straw to the body of the pinwheel by pushing the wire through the tube. Push the flower through the wire as well, and bend the end of the wire into a loop.

Joy   Completed

★★ 107

Cone-Head Pinwheel

Let the wind blow!
Let's run and make the pinwheel spin fast!

Two sheets of 30 × 15 cm, double-sided origami paper

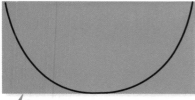

Draw a curve on the paper and cut along the line, as shown.

Apply glue to the shaded area; curl the half-moon shape into a cone and glue into place.

Joy   Completed

Cut slits along the base and make a series of consecutive folds all around the base of the cone, as shown.

Insert the thin role into the cone.

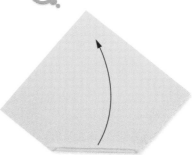

Roll up a 15 × 15 cm sheet of double-sided origami paper along the diagonal.

Decorate the cone with stickers.

Star Pinwheel

This is a pinwheel made by folding a cup.
Use nice colors to make it prettier!

Six sheets of 15 × 15 cm, double-sided origami paper

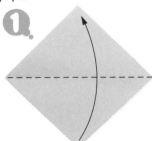

Fold in half on a diagonal.

Make a fold from the bottom right corner to the dot on the opposite edge.

Bring the bottom left corner.

Fold and reverse fold to make a cup.

Fold the top layer of the upper corner inwards to create a pocket.

Using various colored paper, make five more of these pockets.

Apply glue to the shaded area and slide it into another pocket, as shown.

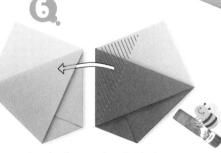

Repeat this five more times.

Shape after all pockets are glued together.

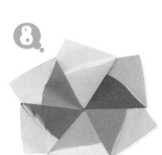

Flip the model over and insert a stick into it.

Joy   Completed

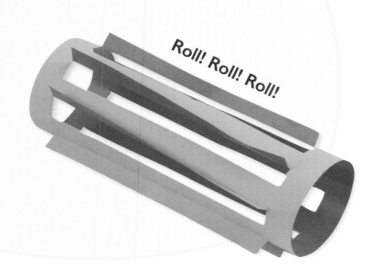

Roller

Place it on the floor and blow on it. It will roll!

Roll! Roll! Roll!

One sheet of 15 × 15 cm,
double-sided origami paper

1.

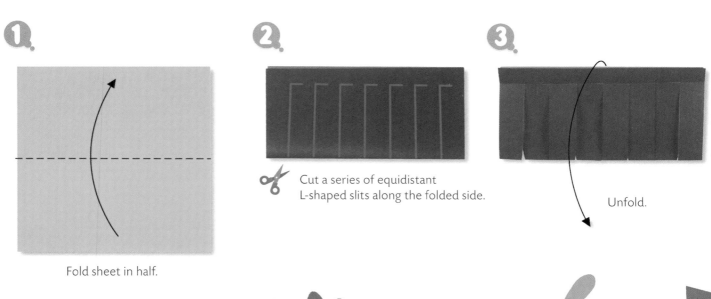

Fold sheet in half.

2.

✂ Cut a series of equidistant
L-shaped slits along the folded side.

3.

Unfold.

5. Apply glue to the shaded area and attach it to the opposite end to create a roll.

4. Fold down each of the flaps, as shown.

Completed

Ball-Riding Pierrot

Hang the clown from a string, and he'll roll around.

Shoes

Two sheets of 15 × 15 cm, double-sided origami paper

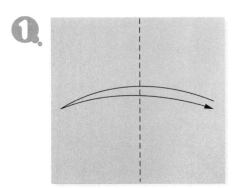

1. Fold the sheet in half and unfold.

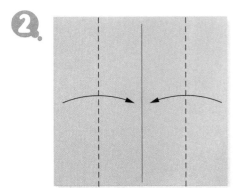

2. Fold both sides to the centerline.

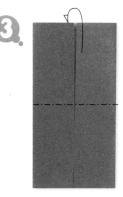

3. Fold in half towards the rear.

4.

The shoe is completed.

Make two of these.

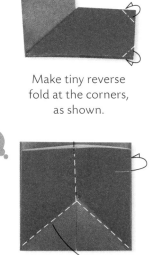

Gather and fold the upper layer while reverse-folding the back sheet in half.

6. Make tiny reverse fold at the corners, as shown.

 112 ★★

Clown

1.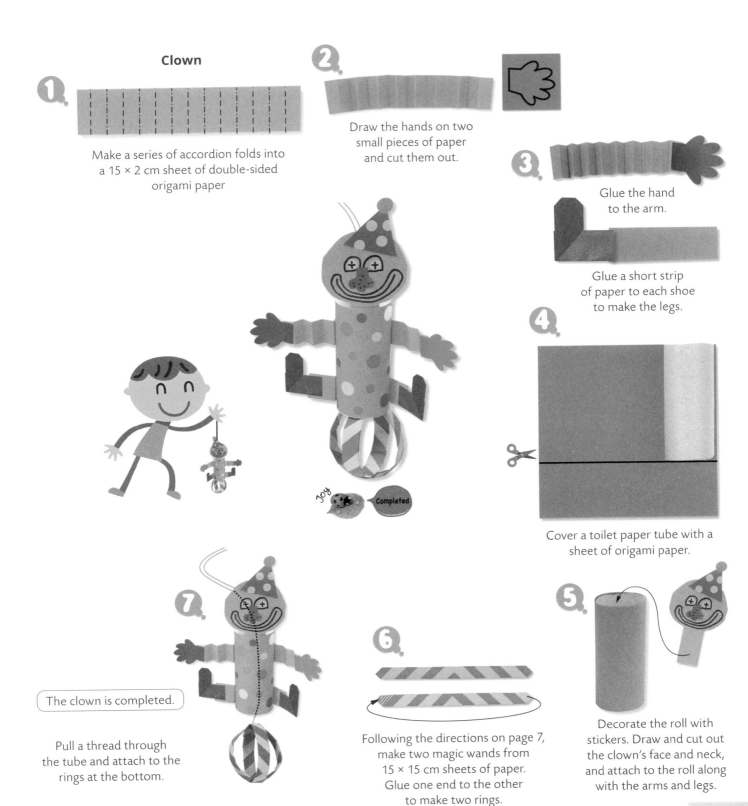

Make a series of accordion folds into a 15 × 2 cm sheet of double-sided origami paper

2.

Draw the hands on two small pieces of paper and cut them out.

3.

Glue the hand to the arm.

Glue a short strip of paper to each shoe to make the legs.

4.

Cover a toilet paper tube with a sheet of origami paper.

5.

Decorate the roll with stickers. Draw and cut out the clown's face and neck, and attach to the roll along with the arms and legs.

6.

Following the directions on page 7, make two magic wands from 15 × 15 cm sheets of paper. Glue one end to the other to make two rings. Glue the loops together as shown.

7.

The clown is completed.

Pull a thread through the tube and attach to the rings at the bottom.

Joy   Completed

Twisted Mobile

Choose different color combinations that match specific locations or warm and cool seasons. Make several twisted mobiles in various hues!

1. Nine or twelve sheets of 15 × 15 cm, double-sided origami paper

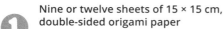

Fold sheet in half.

2.

Cut equidistant slits along the folded edge.

3.

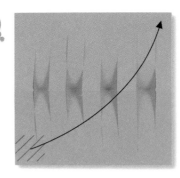

Apply glue to the shaded area and attach it to the opposite corner to create a tube.

4.

Make 8 or 11 more of these tubes to get 3 or 4 elements of the mobile.

5.

Glue the shaded areas together to connect 3 tubes. Repeat 2 or 3 more times.

Attach stickers to the end of each tube. Make a tiny hole in the top of the mobile, pull a thread or fishing line through, and you'll have a beautiful mobile.

Joy

Completed

Ice Cream Mobile

Make three or more identical cones and attach them to each other. Hang them from a thread at the top to create an ice cream mobile!

Five sheets of 15 × 15 cm, double-sided origami paper

1.

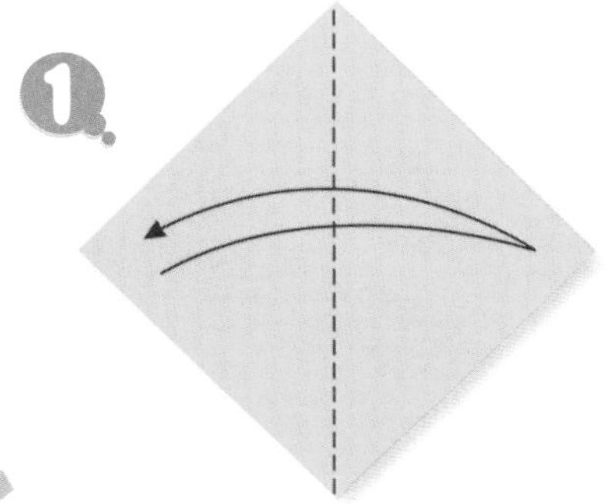

Fold sheet in half along the diagonal, and unfold.

2.

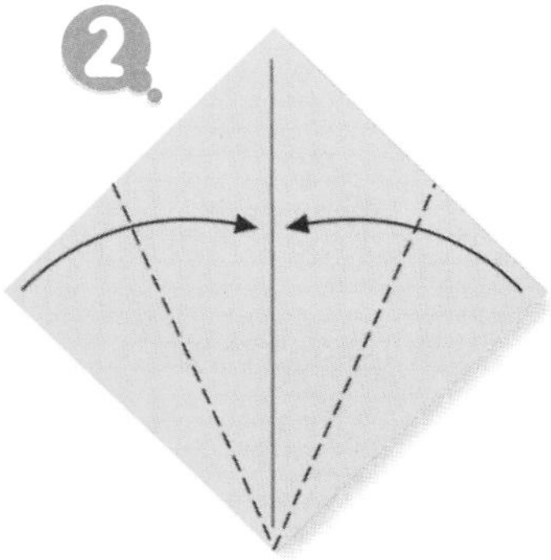

Fold both edges down to the centerline, as shown.

3.

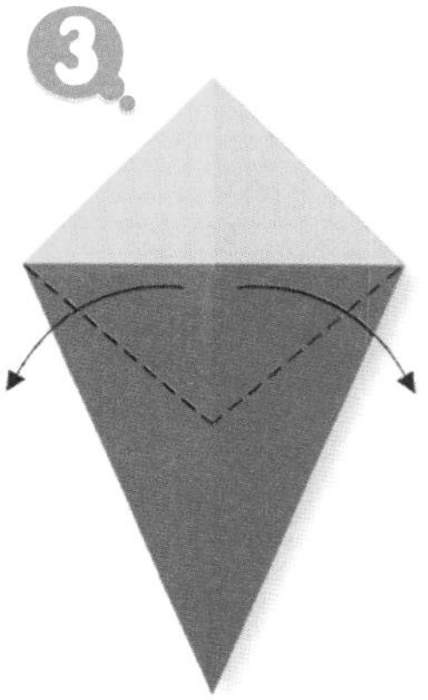

Fold the inner corners outward, as shown.

Wow! This is ice cream cone is delicious!

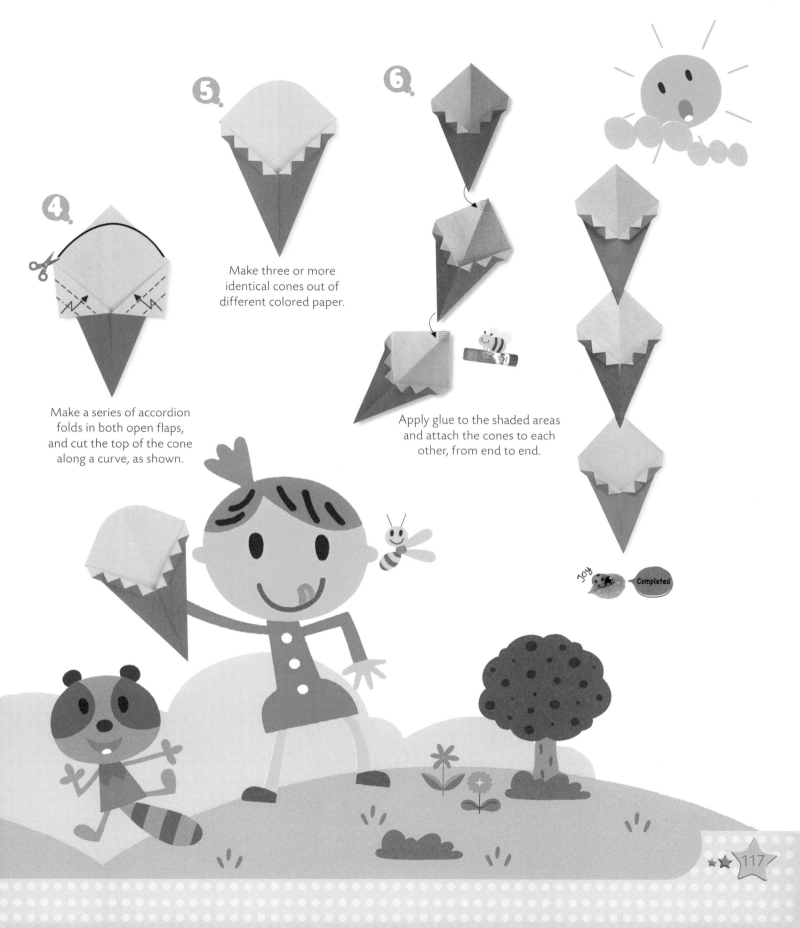

4. Make a series of accordion folds in both open flaps, and cut the top of the cone along a curve, as shown.

5. Make three or more identical cones out of different colored paper.

6. Apply glue to the shaded areas and attach the cones to each other, from end to end.

Joy · Completed

117

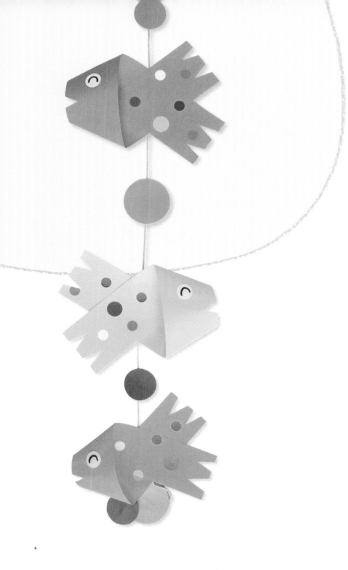

Fish Mobile

Use a narrow rectangular sheet to make this fun fish mobile.

You can do it!

Three sheets of 27 × 4 cm origami paper in different colors

1.

Snip the edges, as shown.

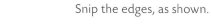

2.

Cross the two ends and glue in place, as shown.

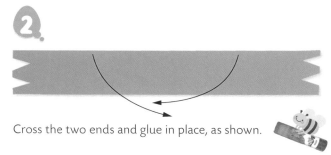

Joy Completed

3.

Cut a little mouth out at one end, and decorate the fish with stickers.

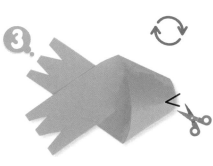

Cube Mobile 1

This one may seem difficult at first, but once you get the hang of it, you'll have lots of fun. It looks great too!

Six sheets of both 7.5 × 7.5 cm and 10 × 10 cm, double-sided origami paper

1.

Fold and unfold, as shown.

You can decorate the surfaces with round or numerical stickers (1-6) to make dice.

2.

Fold the upper and lower edge of the sheet down to the centerline.

3.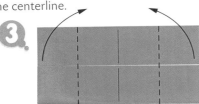

Fold both sides up, as shown.

4.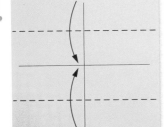

Make six of these.

5.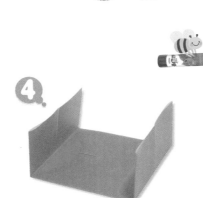

Glue them to each other, as shown.

6.

You will need six to create the cube.

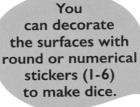

Cube Mobile 2

Fold this cube to create a colorful mobile!

Six sheets of 7.5 × 7.5 cm and 10 × 10 cm, double-sided origami paper for two cubes of different sizes.

1.

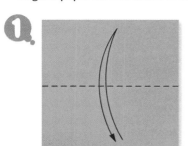

Fold sheet in half, and unfold.

2.

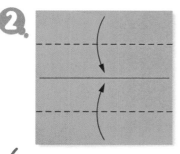

Fold upper and lower edge to centerline.

3.

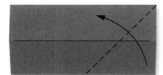

Make a fold from the bottom right corner to the top edge.

4.

Make a fold from the top left corner to the bottom edge.

5.

Make six of these.

6.

Insert the corner of one into the fold of the other, following the direction of the arrow, as shown.

7.

Repeat with the next folded sheet.

8.

Insert all the folded sheets into each other in the same manner.

9.

Complete the cube, as shown.

Joy — Completed

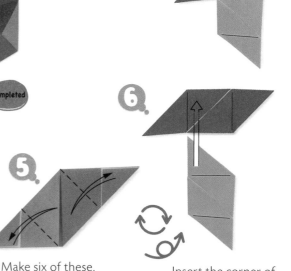

Mobile Hood

Seven sheets of 18 × 18 cm, double-sided origami paper

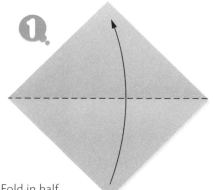

1. Fold in half along the diagonal.

2. Fold the triangle in half, and unfold.

3. Fold right corner up to left edge, as shown.

4. Fold the top corner down and insert top layer into fold.

5. Fold seven sheets in this way.

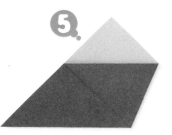

6. Slip the corner of one folded sheet into the fold of another, following the direction of the arrow.

7. Fold up the little corner and glue into place.

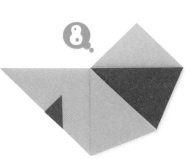

8. Insert the other sheets into one another, one by one.

9.

Following the instructions on page 120, fold pieces of paper around the edge to create a beautiful mobile.

Joy Completed

Lantern Mobile

 **Lantern mobile**

One sheet of 15 × 15 cm, double-sided origami paper

1.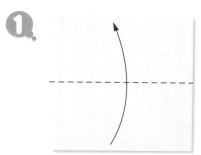

Fold sheet in half.

2.

Cut equidistant slits along the folded edge, as shown.

3.

Unfold.

4.

Apply glue to the shaded edge, and attach it to the opposite edge, as shown.

 **Loop**

Make a mobile for a special occasion!

1.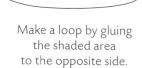

Make a loop by gluing the shaded area to the opposite side.

Insert one loop into another to make a chain.

 Joy · Completed

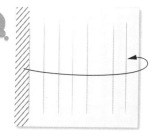

 Joy · Completed

You can make several of these and hang them from the mobile hood on page 121.

Garland

Make a garland for a birthday or Christmas party, or simply to decorate any interior!

Several sheets of 15 × 15 cm, double-sided origami paper

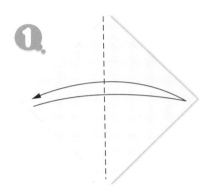

1. Fold sheet along the diagonal, and unfold.

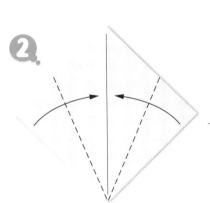

2. Fold sides down to centerline.

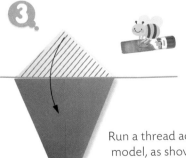

3. Run a thread across the model, as shown, then glue the top corner down over the thread.

4. Fold more sheets in the same way, and string them next to each other to create the garland.

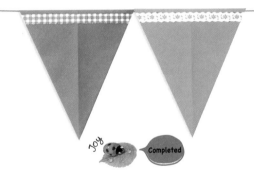

Connect them to each other for decoration.

Joy — Completed

Chapter 6
Chameleon Toys

Paper folding is becoming popular again!
After more than 20 years, I am making a comeback as a paper folding artist
Whenever you encounter something that seems difficult or
impossible, try to do it anyway!
Challenges can be turned into unlimited possibilities!

Let's challenge ourselves with unlimited possibilities!

Let's challenge ourselves with unlimited possibilities!
Whenever I conduct a paper-folding class,
I say things such as, "My friends, take a look at this."
Of course, nobody pays attention to me.
But when I cry out, "My little ones!"
then everyone looks at me.
They know they're not little ones.
It's interesting that such things make children pay attention.
Try not to force our children into a world that we adults
believe they belong in. Instead, allow their own ideas to flow
and let them hold on to their innocence and vitality.
Now, let's travel together to a world of paper folding,
in which infinite changes are possible, shall we?

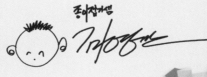

Tulip

This is a simple model. Make tulips out of various types of paper to create your own beautiful flower garden!

All our friends are pretty!

Flower

One sheet of 15 × 15 cm, double-sided origami paper

1.

Fold sheet in half across one diagonal and unfold. Fold sheet across the other diagonal.

2.

Fold both bottom corners up, as shown.

The flower is completed.

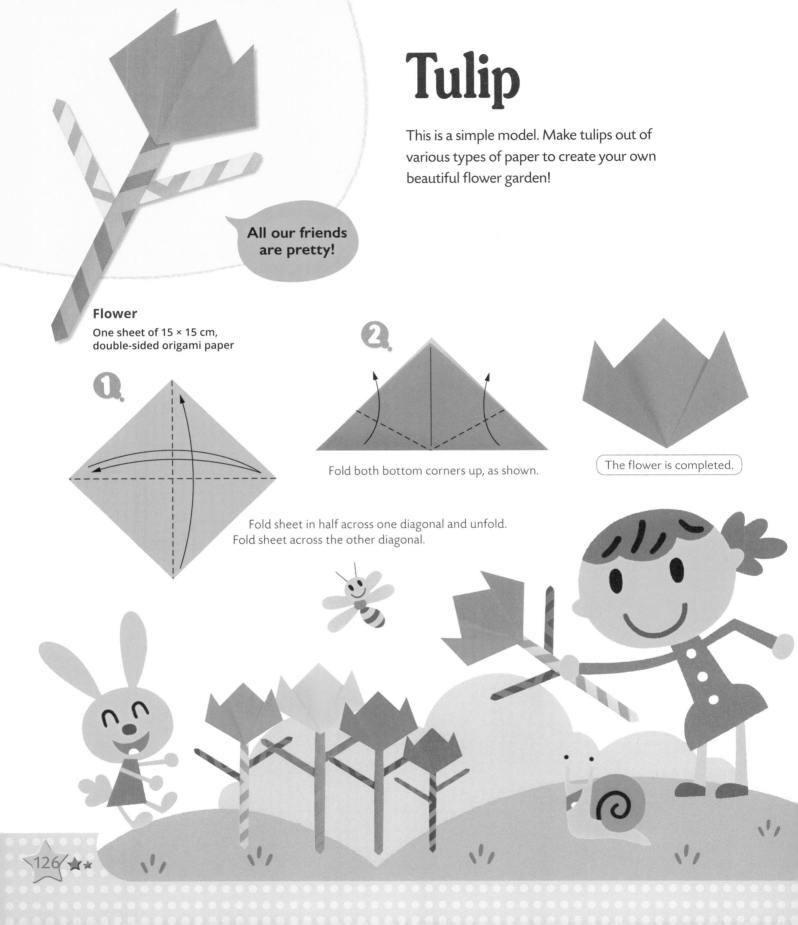

Stem

One sheet of 15 × 15 cm, and two sheets of 7.5 × 7.5 cm, double-sided origami paper

1.

Following the instructions on page 7, make one magic wand with the larger sheet, and two with the smaller sheets. Apply glue to the shaded areas and attach the little wands to the big one, as shown in step **2**.

2.

Joy

Completed

The stem is completed.

Apply glue to the shaded area, and stick the flower on.

★★ 127

The flower goes round and round. It's fun!

Fun Flower

Throw the tulip upward. It will fall while making turns!

One sheet of 7.5 × 7.5 cm, double-sided origami paper

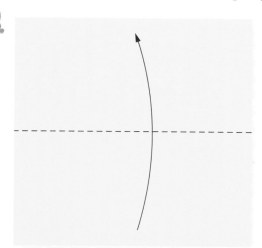

1. Fold sheet in half.

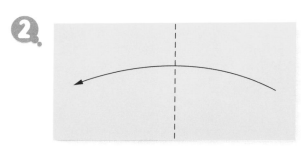

2. Fold in half again.

4. Decorate the flower with a face.

3. Draw the petals of a flower and cut it out.

5. One sheet of 18 × 7 cm, double-sided origami paper

Fold sheet in half.

6. Draw the leaf on the folded sheet, cut it out, and unfold.

7. Unfolded shape.

Toss the flower up in the air and it will twist and turn as it comes down.

Use a clip to hold the stem and leaves in place. Decorate the stem with stickers.

8. One sheet of 2 x 15 cm, double-sided origami paper

Cut a stem out of paper. Fold the two leaves slightly on a diagonal, insert and glue the stem between them, as shown.

Magic Flower 1

A simple model for kids.
Make one for each of your friends!

Six sheets of 15 × 15 cm, double-sided origami paper

1.

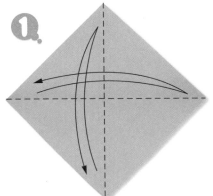

Fold sheet and unfold along both diagonals.

2.

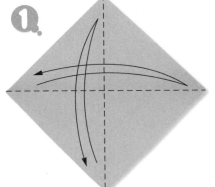

Fold top and bottom corners to centerline.

3.

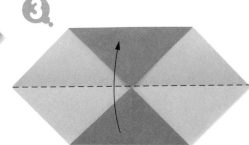

Fold in half lengthwise.

4.

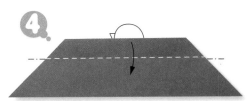

Fold the front layer outward and do the reverse on the back layer.

5.

Fold in half.

6.

Fold four sheets of various colors in this way.

It's easy, isn't it? You can do it, can't you?

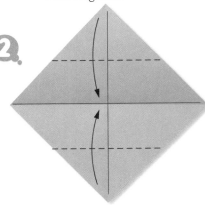

7.

Attach these petals to each other with glue, as shown.

8.

The flower is completed.

9.

Following the instructions on page 7, make two magic wands.

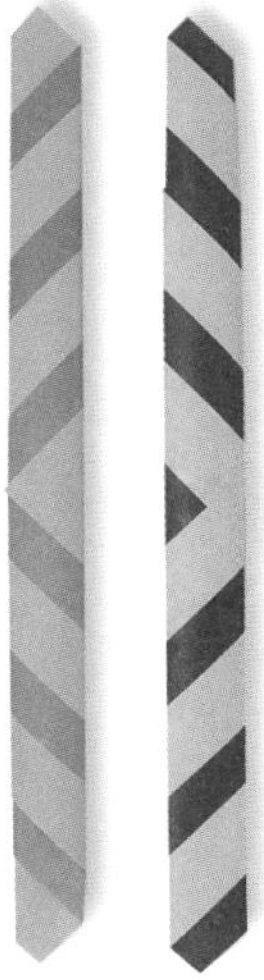

10.

Close the ring of petals. Attach the two wands by gluing them into the folded pockets of the last two petals.

Joy Completed

Open and close the wands to make the magic flower open and close.

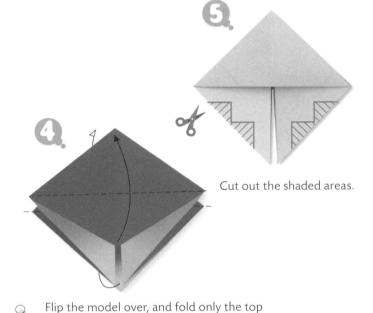

Magic Flower 2

A flower that can be folded and unfolded!

Six sheets of 15 × 15 cm, double-sided origami paper

1.

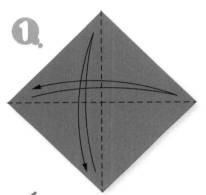

Fold and unfold sheet along both diagonals.

2.

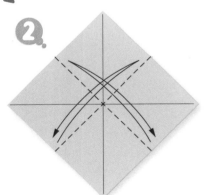

Flip the sheet over, and repeat step **1**.

3.

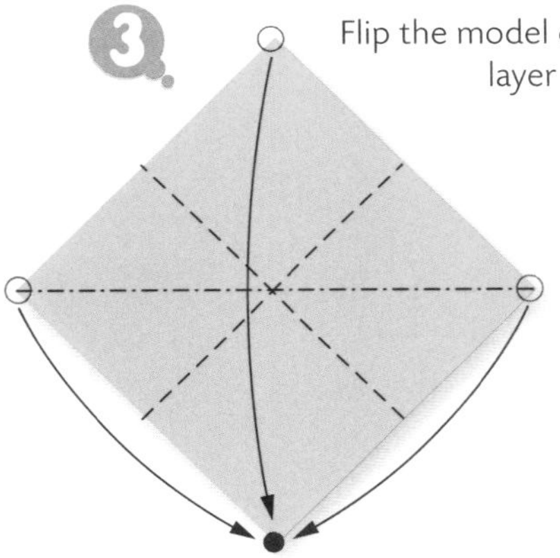

Fold sheet in half from top to bottom, then fold the corners on either side to the dot at the bottom.

4.

Flip the model over, and fold only the top layer back to the top.

5.

Cut out the shaded areas.

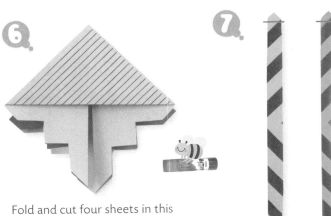

6. Fold and cut four sheets in this manner. Apply glue to the shaded area to overlap them.

7. Following the instructions on page 7, make two magic wands. Snip the ends.

8.  Apply glue to the shaded area, and attach the magic wand to it. Flip the model over and do the same on the other side.

Joy

Completed

You've worked hard today!

Thanks! Love you!

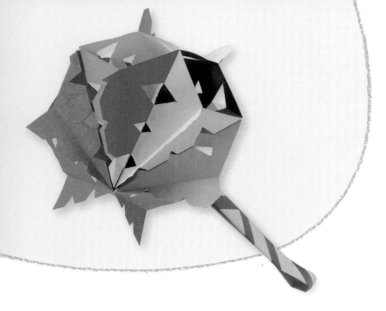

Chameleon Flower

The flower turns out differently depending on how the sheets are cut. Make a variety!

Six sheets of 15 × 15 cm, double-sided origami paper

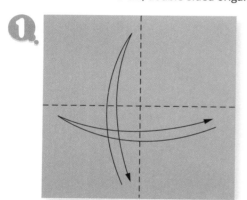

1.

Fold sheet in half and unfold.

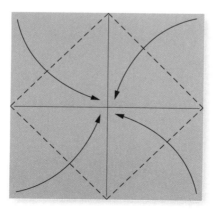

2.

Fold each corner down to the center.

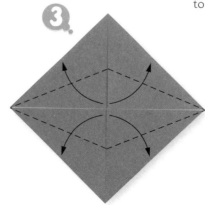

3.

Fold the inside corners out, along the angle shown.

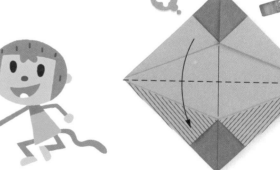

4.

Apply glue to the shaded area, then fold in half and press to attach firmly.

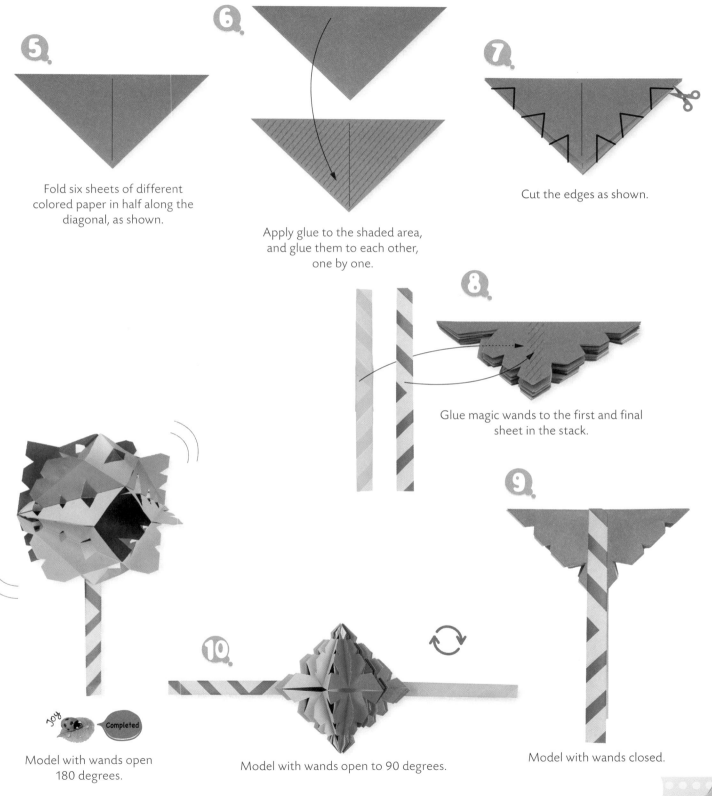

5. Fold six sheets of different colored paper in half along the diagonal, as shown.

6. Apply glue to the shaded area, and glue them to each other, one by one.

7. Cut the edges as shown.

8. Glue magic wands to the first and final sheet in the stack.

9. Model with wands closed.

10. Model with wands open to 90 degrees.

Joy · Completed

Model with wands open 180 degrees.

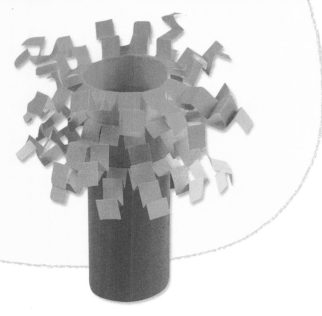

Fountain

Shake it to make it flutter!

Three sheets of 15 × 15 cm, double-sided origami paper

Roll the sheet, glue the shaded area, and attach to the opposite end to make a cylinder.

Make two slightly smaller cylinders the same way.

Insert them into each other, as shown.

4. Once you've inserted them into each other, cut equidistant slits around the circumference, as shown.

5. Appearance after cutting slits.

6. Make a series of accordion folds in each strip.

7. Pull the two inner cylinders partly out of the larger one, as shown.

Here's a present for you!

How pretty! Thank you!

Wow! It looks like a fountain!

Joy Completed

Curly Hair-Do

Cut up a cylinder to create a unique hair-do. Make it with different faces to represent your friends and relatives!

Mom permed her hair!

Joy  Completed

Three sheets of 15 × 15 cm, double-sided origami paper

1.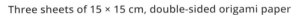

Make three cylinders as in steps **2** and **3** for the Fountain on page 136. Insert them into each other.

2.

Once you've inserted them into each other, cut equidistant slits around the circumference, as shown.

3.

Pull the inner cylinder slightly out of the larger one, as shown.

4.

Curl the strips, and add a face.

Tottering Robot

Tottering, tottering! The robot is tottering! Make many different ones in various colors with different expressions.

1.

Two sheets of double-sided origami paper, one in yellow and one, slightly larger, in blue

Fold along lines, as shown.

2.

Glue along the shaded area, as shown.

3.

The head is completed.

4.

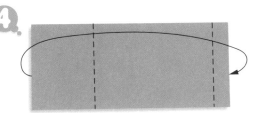

Fold blue sheet along dotted lines, then curl paper over and glue ends.

5.

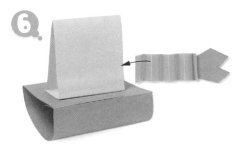

Use glue to attach head to body.

6.

Decorate the head and body. Make a series of accordion folds in two narrow strips of paper to create arms, then glue them to both sides of head.

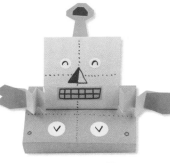

Completed

My Unique Robot 1

One sheet of 14 × 22 cm, double-sided origami paper

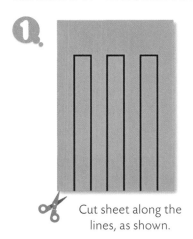

1. Cut sheet along the lines, as shown.

2. Fold the prongs back to make the robot stand.

3. Decorate the robot's body as in the picture, and attach a face.

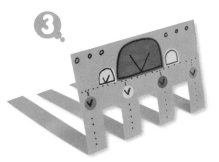

4. Make a series of accordion folds in 13 × 2 cm strips of paper.

5.

Cut out little hands and add them to the arms, then glue the arms to the body.

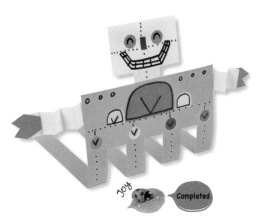

Joy Completed

My Unique Robot 2

1. Two sheets of 25 × 2 cm, double-sided origami paper

Fold along the dotted lines.

2.

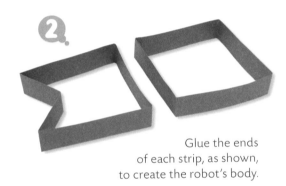

Glue the ends of each strip, as shown, to create the robot's body.

3.

Cut a face out of paper and decorate as shown. Use glue to attach the head and the arms to the body.

4. Make two arms out of two strips of 13 × 2 cm, double-sided origami paper.

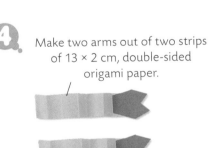

Make a series of accordion folds in each strip. Cut out two hands and glue them to the end of each arm.

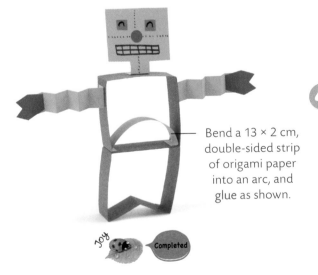

Bend a 13 × 2 cm, double-sided strip of origami paper into an arc, and glue as shown.

Flower Bracelet

If you make it small, you can wear it like a ring.
If you make it big, you can wear it like a bracelet.
Make a special flower bracelet for yourself and a friend!
If you both wear them, your friendship will last forever!

Dear friend, here's a gift for you! Ta-da!

Flower
One sheet of 7.5 × 7.5 cm, single-sided origami paper

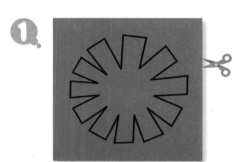

Draw a flower in the sheet and cut it out.

Cut out a small circle and glue it over the shaded area in the center of the flower.

The flower is completed.

Ring

One short strip of double-sided origami paper

1.

Glue one end of a short strip of double-sided origami paper to the other.

2.

The ring is completed.

3.

Following the instructions on page 7, make a magic wand out of a 15 × 15 cm sheet of double-sided origami paper. Glue the ring in the center, as shown.

4.

Glue one end of the wand to the other to make a bracelet, then glue the flower to the shaded area on the ring.

Joy   Completed

Thank you so much!

Here's a present for you!

Flower Bouquet

Make several flowers and place them in a pretty vase. Your home will be full of flowers year round!

Three sheets of 7.5 × 7.5 cm, single-sided origami paper
Four sheets of 3.75 × 5 cm, single-sided origami paper
Three sheets of 4 × 4 cm, single-sided origami paper

1.

Layer the sheets on top of each other, draw the parts of the flower, and cut them out.

2.

Glue the different parts of the flowers together, as shown.

3.

Following the instructions on page 7, make a magic wand out of a 15 × 15 cm sheet of double-sided origami paper, and snip both ends.

Here's a pretty bouquet that I made!

Hey, Raccoon, you must like me don't you? Thanks!

You can make a vase or flowerpot out
of a paper cup or empty toilet-paper roll.

4

Fold a short section (the length of your nail)
on one end of the magic wand.

5

Apply glue to the shaded area and attach the flower.
Glue the leaf to the middle of the wand, as shown.

Joy   Completed

Magic Notebook

Using a soft and brightly colored crayon, draw a funny face on your notebook!

Two sheets of 20 × 20 cm, double-sided origami paper

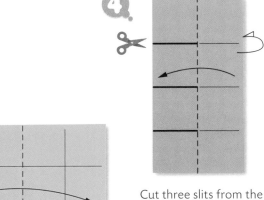

Model when unfolded.

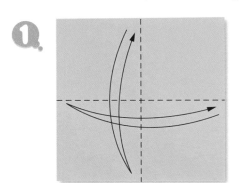

1.

Fold sheet in half and unfold in both directions.

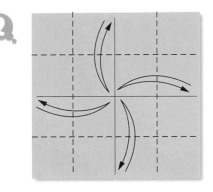

2.

Fold each side of square towards the centerline, then unfold, as shown.

3.

Fold in half.

4.

Cut three slits from the folded edge to the centerline, as shown. Fold the uncut edges back.

6.

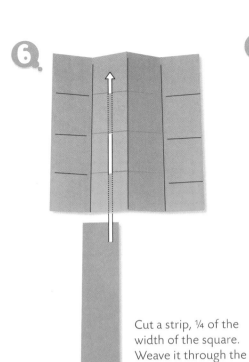

Cut a strip, ¼ of the width of the square. Weave it through the slits as shown.

7.

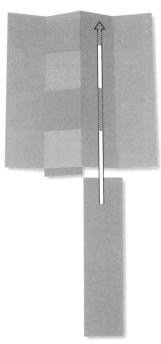

Repeat with another strip.

8.

Decorate the inside of the notebook.

9.

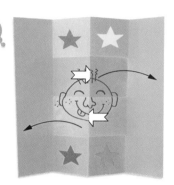

Once you decorate it, unfold it in the direction of the arrow in the picture.

11.

Decorate the unfolded side.

10.

Unfolded shape.

Repeat steps **9** and **10** and the picture will change in an interesting manner.

Roaring Car 1 & 2

Make a car and play a traffic signal game.
Our friends, you observe traffic signals, right?
Move it for green and stop it for red!

 Roaring Car 1

One sheet of 15 × 15 cm, double-sided origami paper

1.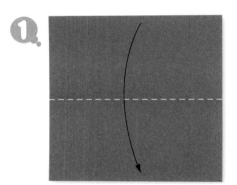

Fold sheet in half.

2.

Fold in half again, lengthwise, and unfold.

3.

Fold the top layer of the bottom up towards the crease made in step **2**.

4.

Folded shape.

5.

Flip model over. Fold down corners to crease line, as shown.

6.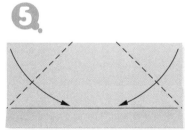

Fold bottom edge up, as shown.

7.

Cut circles out of paper, and attach them as tires to the car. Draw windows.

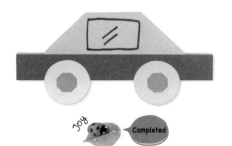

Joy — Completed

Roaring Car 2

Two sheets of 15 × 15 cm,
double-sided origami paper

Top part

 1.

Fold sheet in half.

 1. ### Bottom part

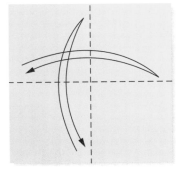

Fold sheet in half, then unfold.

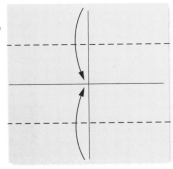 **2.**

Fold top and bottom edges
to the centerline.

2.

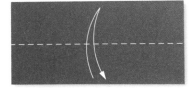

Fold in half again lengthwise,
and unfold.

5.

Flip model to the other side.

Cut windows and tires out
of paper and attach.

3.

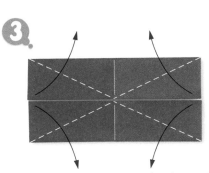

Make two creases across the diagonal of
the rectangle. Fold all four corners of the
sheet in the direction of the arrows.

3.

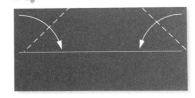

Fold the top corners down as shown.

4.

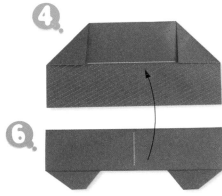 **6.**

Apply glue to the shaded area,
and attach the bottom of the car
to the top.

5.

Fold the projecting corners
at the bottom slightly inward.

4.

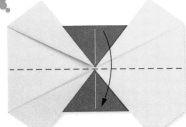

Fold entire model in half
lengthwise.

3-D Car

Create a fantastic 3-D car simply by folding paper!

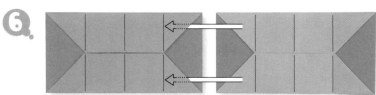

6.

Fold two sheets in this manner, and insert one into the other, as shown.

Top of Car

Two sheets of 15 × 15 cm, double-sided origami paper

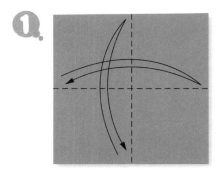

1.

Fold sheet in half in both directions, and unfold.

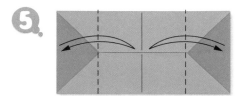

5.

Fold side edges to the centerline, then unfold.

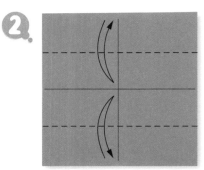

2.

Fold top and bottom edges to the centerline, and unfold.

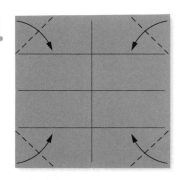

3.

Fold all four corners down to the creases made in step **2**.

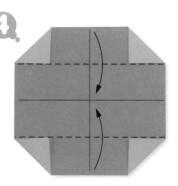

4.

Fold bottom and top edges to the centerline.

7.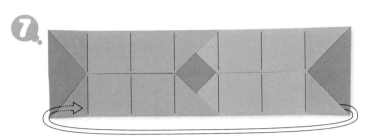

Tuck one end into the other and bend to create a rectangular frame.

8.

The top part is completed.

Base of Car

Two sheets of 15 × 15 cm, double-sided origami paper

6.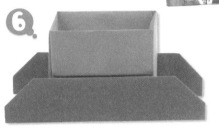

Glue the two sides of the base on either side of the rectangular frame, as shown. Decorate with tires and windows.

Joy   Completed

1.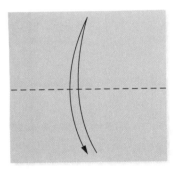

Fold sheet in half and unfold.

5.

The body is completed.

Fold two sheets in this way.

2.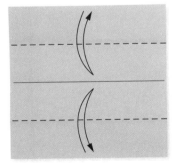

Fold top and bottom edges to the centerline, and unfold.

3.

Fold top and bottom to centerline.

4.

Make reverse folds in both top corners, folding them inward.

UFO

Fling the UFO and it will fly with a swoosh!

Eight sheets of 15 × 15 cm, double-sided origami paper

1.

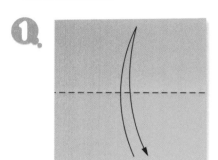

Fold sheet in half and unfold.

2.

Fold the bottom and top corner on the left side down to the centerline.

3.

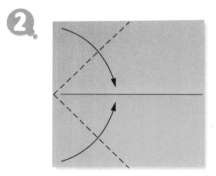

Fold sheet in half along central crease.

4.

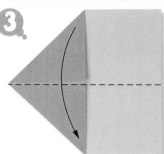

Make an inverse fold with the top right corner, folding inward.

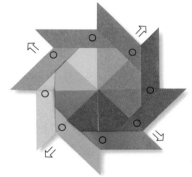

Pull each projecting corner outwards, following the directions of the arrows. The center will open up into a ring.

The ring is completed.

Play a ring-tossing game!

5.

Fold eight differently colored sheets in this way.

7.

Continue inserting one piece into the next.

6.

Insert one piece into another, folding down the projecting tab.

Refreshing Fan

Experiment with various colors.
Use cool, similar, or contrasting colors!

Eight sheets of 15 × 15 cm, double-sided origami paper

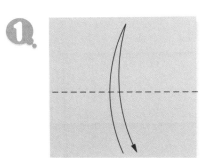

Fold sheet in half and unfold.

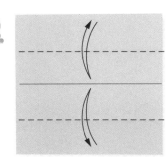

Fold top and bottom edges to the centerline, and unfold.

3. Make a series of accordion folds from top to bottom.

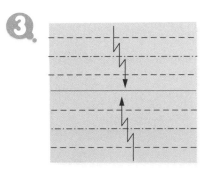

Apply glue to the shaded area and fold the folded sheet in half.

5. Do this with each of the eight sheets, then glue them to each other, one by one.

7. Attach the two wands to both ends of the fan, as shown.

6. Following the instructions on page 7, make two magic wands.

Joy   Completed

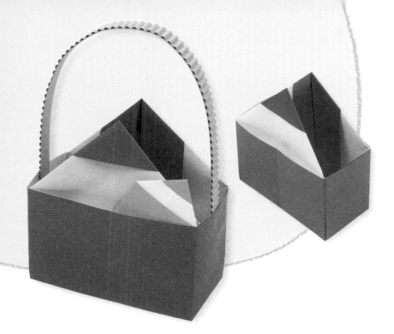

Pencil Holder

Put candies or chocolate in the basket on holidays like Easter or Valentine's Day!

Box

Two sheets of 15 × 15 cm, double-sided origami paper

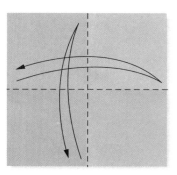

Fold sheet in half in both directions and unfold.

Fold several of these and attach them to each other to make a secret jewelry box!

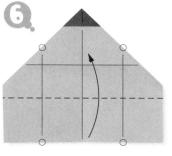

6.

Fold bottom edge to top, making the circles in the diagram align.

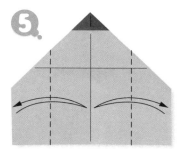

5.

Flip model over. Fold side edges to centerline and unfold.

2.

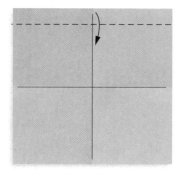

Fold top edge down about 1.5 centimeters.

3.

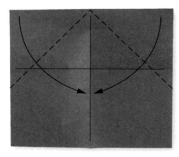

Flip model over. Fold corners of folded edge down to the centerline.

4.

Model after fold is made.

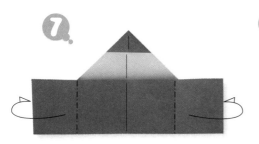

Fold the two side flaps to the rear.

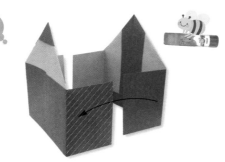

Repeat steps **7**-**7** with another sheet.
Glue the shaded areas on the flap (on either side)
and attach the two halves to create the box.

The box is completed.

Base

**One sheet of 15 × 15 cm,
single-sided origami paper**

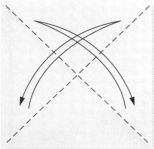

Fold sheet along both
diagonals and unfold.

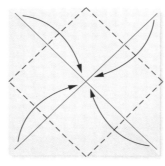

Fold all four corners down
to the center.

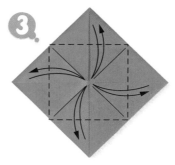

Fold each corner to the center
again, and unfold.

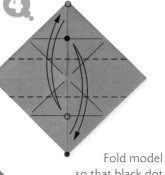

Fold model
so that black dot
meets black dot;
unfold. Fold model
so that circle meets
circle; unfold.

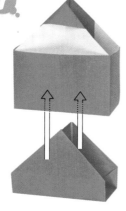

Slip the box over
the base.

Push the paper out along
the creases to make it
3-dimensional.

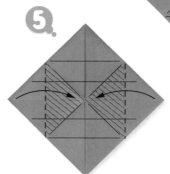

Fold side corners
to the center,
and glue in place.

Our Village

Draw windows, entrances, and chimneys.
Make several homes to create a village!

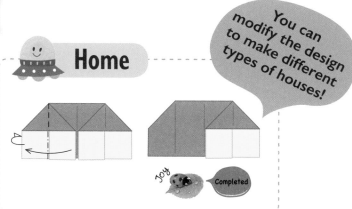

You can modify the design to make different types of houses!

Home

Joy · Completed

Our Home

One sheet of 15 × 15 cm, double-sided origami paper

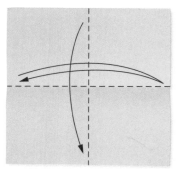

Fold and unfold the sheet vertically,
then fold in half horizontally.

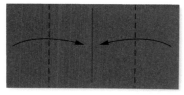

Fold both sides to the centerline.

Fold inside corners down,
as shown.

Joy · Completed

Cut out and glue on windows,
entrances, and chimneys.

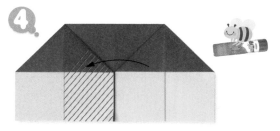

Apply glue to the shaded area, bend the back of
the house to make it three-dimensional, and slip
the glued area beneath the right flap to attach.

Piano and House with Chimney

The house has been transformed into a piano!
Let's think about different ways to change a house!

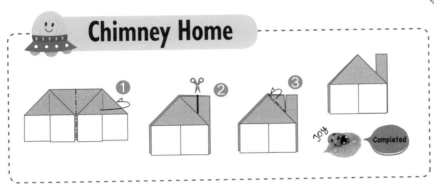

Chimney Home

One sheet of 15 × 15 cm, double-sided origami paper

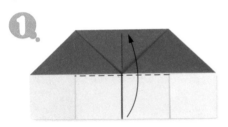

①
Follow instructions for the house up to step ④ on page 156.

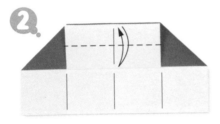

②
Fold the top edge down to the centerline, and unfold.

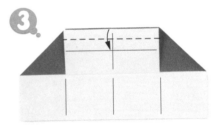

③
Fold the top edge down to the crease that you just made.

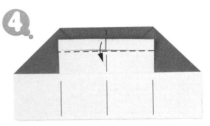

④
Fold the top folded edge over on itself again.

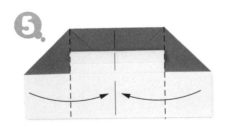

⑤
Fold the two sides in to make the piano three dimensional.

Draw the keyboard.

Christmas Tree and Little Santa Claus

Make a Christmas tree and Santa Claus and let Mom and Dad help you decorate them. Present them as gifts to your grandparents. They'll be delighted!

Ta-da! Santa Claus is coming!

Five sheets of 15 × 15 cm, double-sided origami paper

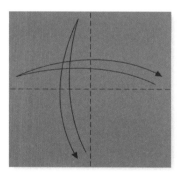

Fold sheet in half and unfold in both directions.

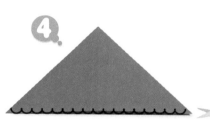

Fold four sheets in this manner.

Cut a scalloped edge with scissors.

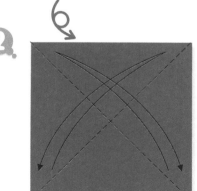

Fold sheet in half and unfold along both diagonals.

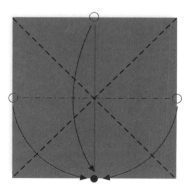

Fold top to bottom, along the line for a triangle pocket (see page 16).

6. Insert the folded sheets into each other so that they overlap, as shown.

7. Following the instructions on page 7, make a magic wand. Snip its edges.

8. Apply glue to the shaded area and insert it into the base of the tree.

Insert the trunk of the tree into a paper cup.

Santa's face

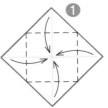

1 Fold all four corners to the center.

2 Unfold one of the corners.

3 Fold the entire model in half from top to bottom, as shown.

4 Fold each of the corners down, as shown.

5 Fold the corner down along the crease, as shown.

6 Flip model over, and stick the corner into Santa's hat.

7 Attach the hat to the face, and glue to paper cup.

Hat of Santa Claus

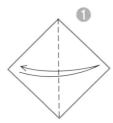

1 Fold sheet in half along diagonal and unfold.

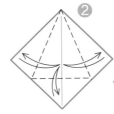

2 Fold the two sides in as shown and unfold; fold bottom up and unfold.

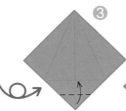

3 Flip model over.

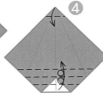

4 Roll model up with a series of folds.

5 Fold both sides back.

6 Hat after all folds completed.

100 Paper Folding Projects © Snake SA 2017

www.nuinui.ch

nuinui ® is a trademark of Snake SA

© 2017 Snake SA
Chemin du Tsan du Péri, 10
3971 Chermignon
Switzerland

ISBN 978 2 88935 811 3
Printed in Poland

Translation: Irina Oryshkevich

Licensed Edition of the Work
100 Paper folding projects
© 2017, Jong le Nara Co., Ltd.
7F Jong le Nara Bldg. 166 Jangchungdan-ro,
Jung-gu, Seoul, Korea Zip code #04606
www.jongienara.com
All Rights reserved.
Writer: Kim Young-man
Publisher: Rho Young-hye
Paper Folding Production: Kim Young-sun, Kwak Jeong-hun,
and Park Seon-young
Design: Jung Kyu-il, Han Yeon-jae, Ahn Young-jun,
Kang U-jeong, and Kim Bo-ri
Art: Ahn Jeong-tae, Jong le Nara Design Institute
Production and Marketing: Kook Heun-chul and Choi Jeong-i